Church Alive!

Comparing Church Work
With the Work of the Church

Harold Trammell

Treasure House
An Imprint of
Destiny Image
P.O. Box 310
Shippensburg, PA 17257

"For where your treasure is
there will your heart be also." Matthew 6:21

ISBN 1-56043-820-7

For Worldwide Distribution
Printed in the U.S.A.

Treasure House books are available through these fine distributors outside the United States:

Christian Growth, Inc.
Jalan Kilang-Timor, Singapore 0315

Successful Christian Living
Capetown, Rep. of South Africa

Lifestream
Nottingham, England

Vision Resources
Ponsonby, Auckland, New Zealand

Rhema Ministries Trading
Randburg, South Africa

WA Buchanan Company
Geebung, Queensland, Australia

Salvation Book Centre
Petaling, Jaya, Malaysia

Word Alive
Niverville, Manitoba, Canada

Inside the U.S., call toll free to order:
1-800-722-6774

Dedication

To my loving wife, Denese G. Trammell, whose love for our Lord has been my inspiration. I have been blessed to have her as my companion, buddy, defender, and best friend.

To the officers and members of Mt. Jezreel Baptist Church, Washington, D.C. Their love and support has made serving as pastor a joyous experience.

To the many churches that gave me an opportunity to conduct the Institute with their congregations, and for their many letters and words of encouragement.

Contents

Introduction

Day Five

Introduction

Between 1990 and 1992 my church, the First Baptist Church of Glenarden, became involved in supporting foreign missions financially. Ten percent of our revenue was earmarked for the spread of the gospel outside of the Glenarden community. *Wow!* I thought, *We are doing what the Word tells us do.*

In November 1990, Pastor John K. Jenkins introduced the congregation to something that changed my whole life. It was the "Church Alive Institute," a week of teaching what the "Church" was really supposed to be about.

Reverend Harold Trammell, pastor of the Mount Jezreel Baptist Church, was the lecturer for the Church Alive Institute.

During the Institute, Reverend Trammell clarified the difference between "church work" and "the work of the Church." He challenged the First Baptist family to get busy doing the work of the Church. Reverend Trammell brought this point home through an illustration of two pies.

The first pie was sliced to depict the auxiliaries of the Church (choirs, clubs, circles, boards, etc.). The second pie was sliced to depict the many problems of our society...the world.

Reverend Trammell then asked the piercing question, "What are the clubs, circles, etc., of the first pie doing to reduce the size of the second pie?" The answer was...little or nothing.

The pie illustration showed us that we are so wrapped up and tied up in ourselves that we are neglecting our real purpose: "the work of the Church."

The message of the Church Alive Institute had a profound effect on my life. In fact, it cut right to my heart. The message challenged me to examine how I spent my God-given time, money, and talent.

"Church Alive" was a life-changing experience for me more than I realized at the time of the first Institute.

One month earlier I had accepted my call to the ministry and God had given me a burning desire to help those who were less fortunate than I (the hungry, homeless, disadvantaged, etc.).

In December 1990, my family sponsored a Christmas day dinner for the homeless persons in shelters throughout Prince George's County, Maryland, and for senior citizens. Nearly 70 people were fed. We also prepared bag lunches and took them to the streets of Washington,

D.C., where we fed 50 people. I felt good, but I still believed there was so much more that needed to be done.

During the next ten months I was very active in the prison ministry at Women's Halfway House and at the Horizon House, a juvenile shelter in Chetlenham, Maryland. The church was also very active in carrying out the "work of the Church." I did whatever I could as often as I could, as did many others.

November 1991 rolled around and the Church sponsored "Church Alive II." Everybody was excited about the "work of the Church" that had been done since the first Institute. Each auxiliary gave a report of what it had done, and yes, our report in 1991 was very impressive compared to our report in 1990. You could say that "we had our chest stuck out in pride." But Reverend Trammell hadn't dropped the bomb yet...

Reverend Trammell applauded us for our efforts. He then proceeded to talk about the "Jerusalem Journey." It was only the Church's starting point. Reverend Trammell said that now it was time for us to "go on to Judea."

...and ye shall be witnesses unto Me both in Jerusalem, and in all Judaea... (Acts 1:8).

Judea was beyond the Glenarden community.

What I remember most about the "Church Alive Institutes" was the journey outward we had, and the tips given on "faith" for the journey—strong faith, great faith, active faith, and unwavering faith.

Belynda Gentry, Minister
First Baptist Church of Glenarden

Day One

Part One

The Church of the Called-Out Ones

There are two basic New Testament definitions for the Church. The first definition I want to discuss is found in the Book of Matthew, chapter 16.

> *And I say also unto thee, That thou art Peter, and upon this rock I will build My church; and the gates of hell shall not prevail against it* (Matthew 16:18).

The word *church* in this verse is from the Greek word *ecclesia* (pronounced: ek-kla-see-ah). This refers to the Church as an institution and is best visualized as a living organism rather than as an organization. I like to think of this as a description of the Church within. Just as our individual bodies have a number of members, so does the Church, as the Body of Christ, have many members. Also, just as each of our members is alive and functions according to a specific purpose, so do the members within the Church function and have a purpose.

One becomes a member of the Church through human and divine encounter. The traditional expression is "being born again," and is sometimes referred to as "the new birth." This new birth is brought about when an individual accepts Jesus Christ as his personal Savior. Being born again is not simply an empty confession. It assumes a willing acceptance of Jesus and implies obedience to the concepts He taught.

These concepts form the basis for a process that begins with the new birth. It will be easier to understand the process as a whole by breaking it down into a series of steps or qualities, which are evidence or proof of the process.

Learning About Forgiveness

In the New Testament, there are two Greek words translated as "forgiveness": *aphiemi* and *charizomai*.

1. The primary meaning of *aphiemi* is "to send forth, send away," but it also can carry the meaning of "to remit or forgive." For example, this word appears in Matthew 6:12 (the Lord's Prayer): "And forgive us our debts, as we forgive our debtors." In Matthew 18:27 the master was moved with compassion, loosed his servant, and forgave his debt. There are other examples where sins or debts have been cancelled (see Mt. 9:2,5-6; Rom. 4:7).

In light of these translations, you can see that this word is used to signify the remission of the punishment due to sinful conduct and the deliverance of the sinner from the penalty of divine justice. Another way it is used in translation is to demonstrate the complete removal or remission of the cause of the offense. This remission is based upon the vicarious and propitiatory sacrifice of Christ.

In the Old Testament the sacrifice of atonement and the act of forgiveness are often associated with one another (see Lev. 4:20,26). The prayer offered by Jesus in Matthew 6:12 shows us that human forgiveness is analogous to divine forgiveness. When certain conditions are fulfilled, there is no limitation to Christ's law of forgiveness. Matthew 18:21-22 and Luke 17:3-4 tell us that these conditions are repentance and confession.

2. The Greek word *charizomai* is also translated as "forgiveness" and refers to either divine or human forgiveness. (For examples of divine forgiveness see Ephesians 4:32 and Colossians 2:13; for examples of human forgiveness see Luke 7:42,43.) Its basic meaning is "to bestow a favor unconditionally."

The word *forgiveness* can best be understood to mean "to remove the barrier." Man and God became separated by sin; sin was the barrier between God and man. Man had neither the will nor the ability to remove the barrier. God, through the redemptive act of His Son, Jesus Christ, acted to remove the barrier of sin and to restore man to his original position as a son and an heir of God the Father. Justice was satisfied by the atoning death of Jesus. God cancelled the debt of man and forgave man his sin. Thus the old account was settled.

God's goodness and faithfulness toward His people is strikingly symbolized by His presence in the temple in Jerusalem, which is the "city of the great King." But there is no greater evidence of His love for His creation than His willingness to forgive sin. His forgiveness is extended to those who humbly confess their sins and whose hearts demonstrate genuine repentance.

Moses recorded the ancient testimony of the Israelites' covenant with the Lord when Yahweh (the Lord) proclaimed, "...The Lord, The Lord God, merciful and gracious, longsuffering, and abundant in goodness and truth, keeping mercy for thousands, *forgiving* iniquity and transgression and sin..." (Ex. 34:6-7).

On the basis of this promise, the people dared to submit to Him as His people and to "fear" Him. God's response toward those who confess their sins will be in accordance with His nature and His gracious commitment to His people. He acts according to His word and fulfills His promise to forgive.

Ultimately, this forgiveness was provided through Jesus Christ. He restored the communion with God that had been interrupted by sin. Jeremiah 31:31 begins:

> *Behold, the days come, saith the Lord, that I will make a new covenant with the house of Israel and with the house of Judah: not according to the covenant that I made with their fathers in the day that I took them by the hand to bring them out of the land of Egypt; which My covenant they brake, although I was an husband unto them, saith the Lord: but this shall be the covenant that I will make with the house of Israel; After those days, saith the Lord, I will put My law in their inward parts, and write it in their hearts; and will be their God, and they shall be My people. And they shall teach no more every man his neighbour, and every man his brother, saying, Know the Lord: for they shall all know Me, from the least of them unto the greatest of them, saith the Lord: for I will forgive their iniquity, and I will remember their sin no more* (Jeremiah 31:31-34).

This quotation is a prophetic announcement and definition of the new covenant. It differs from the Mosaic covenant because it has superior benefits. These benefits include the following:

1. God's laws will become inner principles that enable His people to delight in doing His will.
2. God and His people will have intimate fellowship.
3. Sinful ignorance of God will be removed forever.
4. Forgiveness of sins will be an everlasting reality.

Jacob Chamberlain, an early missionary to India, tells of a man who had crawled many agonizing miles on his knees and elbows to bathe in the "sacred stream"—the Ganges. The poor exhausted soul made his prayer to Gunga and then slipped into the water. But he emerged with the same conviction of sin as before. The fear of death still tugged at his heart. Chamberlain then told him the wonderful story of grace and how Christ died on Calvary's cross to rescue needy sinners. With new hope the man staggered to his feet, clasped his hands together, and cried, "Oh, that's what I need! Forgiveness and peace!" The missionary soon led him to accept Jesus as his personal Savior.[1]

Learning About Redemption

There are three Greek words that are often used to express the concept of redemption. Each carries the idea of buying or purchasing something in order to set it free.

---

1.   *Sermon Illustrations for Windows*, by NAVPRESS, P.O. Box 6000, Colorado Springs, CO 80934. Used by permission.

This is the basis for Christian redemption and is the corner-stone of Jesus' sacrificial act of atonement. It was through the price He paid that the debt of sin was satisfied.

1. The first word, *apolutrosis* (pronounced: ap-ol-oo-tro-sis), means "to dismiss for a ransom paid." It is a combination of two root words and it carries the idea of "redemption, a deliverance procured by the payment of a ransom." The key verse in this principle is found in Hebrews 9:12: "Neither by the blood of goats and calves, but by His own blood He entered in once into the holy place, having obtained eternal redemption for us."

2. The second word, *exagorazo* (pronounced: ex-a-gor-azo), means "to buy" or "to buy out." This is used especially of purchasing a slave for the purpose of setting him free. In Galatians 3:13 and 4:5 it is used as a metaphor to confirm the deliverance of Christian Jews from the law and its curse.

3. The third word, *lutroo* (pronounced: lu-troo), means "to release for a ransom." It is often used to demonstrate release, deliverance, or liberation. In the sense of delivering, Luke 24:21 uses this word to describe the release of Israel from the Roman yoke. In a spiritual sense, Titus 2:14 talks of the work of Christ in redeeming men from all iniquity and the bondage of self-will, which rejects the will of God. First Peter 1:18 says that we were redeemed from a vain manner of life or from bondage to tradition. In both instances the death of Christ is stated as the means of "redemption."

In Judaism there is a ceremony called "the redemption of the firstborn." The Book of Numbers lists specific rules for such a redemption, including costs and manner of sacrifices. Legend records a time in pagan history when the firstborn of all families were sacrificed to the gods. Parents could buy back their children from the gods by paying a given price. In effect the parent was buying back something that was once owned, but surrendered in payment for a debt. God, our Father, is buying us back by satisfying a debt that is owed.

Genesis speaks of beginnings—of the heavens and the earth; of light and darkness; of seas and skies; of land and vegetation; of sun, moon and stars; of sea, air, and land animals; of human beings (made in God's own image, the climax of His creative activity); of sin and redemption; of blessing and cursing; of society and civilization; of marriage and family; of art, craft, and industry—the list goes on and on. A key word in Genesis is *account*, which also serves to divide the book into its ten major parts, or accounts, and which include such concepts as birth, genealogy, and history.

The Book of Genesis is foundational for understanding the rest of the Bible. Its message is rich and complex and a list of its main elements produces a succinct outline of the biblical message as a whole. It is primarily a book of relationship, highlighting the relationships between God and nature, God and man, and man and man. It is thoroughly monotheistic and thus supports the Christian belief there is only one God worthy of the name. Monotheism rejects the concepts of polytheism (many gods), atheism (no gods), and pantheism (everything is god). It clearly teaches that the one true God is sovereign over all that exists and by divine election He often exercises His unlimited power to overturn human customs, traditions, and plans. Genesis introduces us to the way God initiates and makes covenants with His chosen people. It demonstrates His love and affirms His faithfulness to them. It also calls upon these same people to promise to love Him and to act faithfully toward Him.

It establishes sacrifice as a substitution of life for life. It gives us the first hint of God's provision for redemption from the forces of evil and it contains the oldest and most profound definition of faith (see Gen. 15:6). The heroes mentioned in Hebrews 11—the New Testament's hall of fame of the faithful—refers to characters in Genesis.

I am reminded of a true story about a past governor of Texas. Governor Neff was speaking to an assembly of convicts at the state penitentiary. He finished by saying that he would remain to listen if any man wanted to speak with him. He further announced that what was said would be held in confidence, so nothing a man might tell him would be used against him.

When the meeting was over, a large group of men remained, many of them life-termers. One by one they told the governor that they were in jail because of a frame-up, an injustice, or a judicial blunder. Each one asked the governor to set him free. Finally, one man came up and said, "Mr. Governor, I just want to say that I am guilty. I did what they sent me here for, but I believe I paid for it. If I were granted the right to go out, I would do everything I could to be a good citizen and prove myself worthy of your mercy." This man the governor pardoned.

So it is with the great God who alone can pardon us and release us from the prison of sin. The one difference between us and the prisoners in the penitentiary is we cannot say that we have paid for any of our transgressions. Still, we can come to God and say, "O God, I just want to say I am guilty. I am a sinner, a rebel against Thy power and Thy justice, but I believe that Jesus Christ paid for my sin. If, in Thy mercy and because of Him, Thou wilt take me out of darkness into light, I will live as one who is alive from the dead." This, of course, is the man whom God will pardon.

Day One

Part Two

The Church of the Called-Out Ones

Learning About Justification

The Greek word *dikaioma* (pronounced: dik-ah'-yo-mah) is a noun that means "an equitable deed" and, by implication, a statute or decision. Underlying statutes or decisions are concepts of judgment, justification, ordinances, and righteousness.

The act of pronouncing righteous justification or acquittal comes from the related verb form *dikaio*, which means "to justify." This verb is used only twice in the New Testament. In both instances the word appears in Paul's letter to the Romans and declares that a person has been acquitted of all guilt. In Romans 4:25 the phrase "for our justification" is literally "because of our justification." Here justification was rendered in spite of our trespasses and was made possible because God accepted Jesus' death as payment for our offense, namely our sin. Paul tells us that Jesus was raised from the dead so we could be justified. His resurrection was evidence of God's acceptance.

In Romans 5:18, the phrase "justification of life" should be understood to mean "justification which results in life" (see also Rom. 5:21). When God justifies the believing sinner based upon Christ's death, He also grants him His free gift of life everlasting.

Beginning with verse 18, Romans 5 reads:

Therefore as by the offense of one judgment came upon all men to condemnation; even so by the righteousness of one the free gift came upon all men unto justification of life. For as by one man's disobedience many were made sinners, so by the obedience of one shall many be made righteous. Moreover the law entered, that the offence might abound. But where sin abounded, grace did much more abound: that as sin hath reigned unto death, even so might grace reign through righteousness unto eternal life by Jesus Christ our Lord (Romans 5:18-21).

When dealing with the Greek language, there are subtleties that occur within the various moods and tenses that are not always apparent in the English translation. For example, Paul uses another form of the Greek verb, in this case *dikaioun*, that also means "to justify." In this sense it has a different meaning from the normal English meaning. If we are to justify ourselves, we must produce reasons to prove that we are entitled to exoneration. On the other hand, if someone else acts to exonerate us, he must produce reasons to prove that we are. Where verbs of this type are used, they do not necessarily mean to prove or to make a person or thing to be something. Instead they deal with the way a person is to be treated as a result of the action.

In the case of our justification through Jesus Christ, God has determined that we should be treated, or accounted or reckoned, as acquitted even though we may not deserve such treatment. When God justifies a sinner, it does not mean that He finds reasons to prove that He was right—far from it. It does not even mean, at this point, that He makes the sinner a good man. It simply means that God treats the sinner as if he had not been a sinner at all. Instead of treating him as if he is a criminal who deserves death, God treats him as a child to be loved. That is what justification means.

Through Christ's sacrifice we are justified and reckoned not as His enemies, but as His friends. We are no longer treated as law breakers who deserve punishment, but as good men who deserve His compassion. That is the very essence of the gospel.

To be justified is to enter into a new relationship with God, a relationship of love, confidence, and friendship, instead of a relationship of separation, enmity, and fear. We no longer go to a God who radiates justice through terrible punishment. We go to a God who radiates forgiveness and redemptive love. Justification is a right relationship between God and man. The man who is made just is the man who is in this right relationship and—here is the supreme point—he is in it not because of anything that he has done, but because of what God has done. He is in this right relationship not because he has meticulously performed the works of the law, but because in utter faith he has cast himself on the amazing mercy and love of God.

Paul, in explaining this concept of justification, uses a number of metaphors to help us understand God's grace and mercy. One such metaphor comes from the courts of law in which a man is on trial before God. If an innocent man appears before a judge, then to treat him as innocent is to acquit him. But man, in his relationship with God, is not innocent. He is guilty. Nevertheless God, in His amazing mercy, treats him, reckons him, and accounts him as if he is innocent. When Paul says, "God justifies the ungodly," he means that God treats the ungodly man as if he had been a good man.

That is what shocked the Jews to the core of their beings. To treat a bad man as if he is good was the sign of a wicked judge. "He that justifieth the wicked...[is an] abomination to the Lord" (Prov. 17:15). "...I will not justify the wicked" (Ex. 23:7). But Paul says that is precisely what God does. How can I know that God is like that? I know because Jesus said so. He came to tell us that God loves us, bad as we are. He came to tell us that, although we are sinners, we are still dear to God. When we discover this truth and believe it, our whole relationship with God changes. We are conscious of our sin, but we no longer live in terror of God and estranged from Him. Penitent and brokenhearted, we come to God like a repentant child coming to his father, to receive His love. We are children, albeit erring children, trusting in our Father's love for forgiveness. We could never have found that right relationship with God if Jesus had not come to live and to die, showing us how wonderfully He loves us.

A second metaphor comes from the idea of sacrifice. Paul tells us that God sent Jesus as One who can win forgiveness for our sins. The Greek word Paul uses to describe this action of Jesus is *hilasterion*. This comes from a verb that means "to propitiate" or "to remove guilt" and refers to atonement through sacrifice. Under the old system, when a man broke the law, he brought a sacrifice. His aim was for the sacrifice to act as a substitute for the punishment due him because of his sin. His sin had placed him in a wrong relationship with God. His sacrifice was to satisfy the penalty for his sin and restore his relationship with God.

Unfortunately, animal sacrifices failed to fully satisfy God's requirements.

For Thou desirest not sacrifice; else would I give it: Thou delightest not in burnt offering (Psalm 51:16).

Wherewith shall I come before the Lord, and bow myself before the high God? Shall I come before Him with burnt offerings, with calves a year old? Will the Lord be pleased with thousands of rams, or with ten thousands of rivers of oil? shall I give my firstborn for my transgression, the fruit of my body for the sin of my soul? (Micah 6:6-7)

Instinctively men felt, once they had sinned, that the paraphernalia of earthly sacrifice could not put matters right. They were aware of their own imperfections and inability to continue without sin.

So Paul says, "Jesus Christ, by His life of obedience and His death of love, made the one sacrifice to God which really and truly atones for sin." He insists that what happened on the cross opens the door to a right relationship with God, a door that every other sacrifice is powerless to open.

A third metaphor deals with slavery. Paul, speaking of the deliverance wrought through Jesus Christ, uses the word *apolutrosis*. It means "a ransoming, a redeeming or a liberating." It implies that man was bound by the power of sin and that Jesus Christ alone could free him from it.

Paul concludes that God, as a just Judge, accepts all who believe in Jesus as justified. Bengel called this concept of Paul's "the supreme paradox of the gospel." The natural way of justice is to say, "God is just, and therefore, condemns the sinner as a criminal." But here we have the great paradox: God is just and somehow, through His incredible, miraculous grace, He sent Jesus to offer that which no man could provide. As a result, God accepts the sinner, not as a criminal, but as a son whom He still loves.

What is the essence of all this? Where is the difference between this way and the old way of the law? The basic difference is this: The way of obedience to the law is concerned with what a man can do in and for himself; the way of grace is concerned with what God can do and has done without man's help. Paul is insisting that nothing we can ever do can achieve the forgiveness of God. Therefore, the way to a right relationship with God does not lie in a frenzied, desperate, doomed attempt to win acquittal by personal performance. It lies in the humble, penitent acceptance of the love and grace that God offers us in Jesus Christ.

Experiments have been made in which people were fitted with special prismatic glasses. These devices caused things to look upside down to the wearer. Vision was so greatly distorted that straight lines appeared to be curved and sharp outlines seemed fringed with color. Within just a few days, however, the unnatural shapes, tinted edges, and inverted landscapes gradually disappeared. The world began to appear normal again, even though the optical devices were still in place. Over time, the brain overcame the distortion and accepted the images as correct.

This adaptability of the physical realm is indeed a blessing. However, in the spiritual arena, the human mind does not function very well. In fact, man is a sinner whose deepest imaginations are evil, and his thought-life produces a world of illusions. He thinks of himself as pure when in reality he is guilty before God. Truly we need God's grace and mercy, that we may repent.

Learning About Repentance

The Greek word behind the concept of repentance is *metamelomai*. It means "to regret" or "to change one's mind and purpose."

The believer has a role to play in the process of growth out of sin and through the process that leads to sanctification. There must be a change in man's thinking. Man's relationship to man is based upon one's actions. Man's relationship to God is based upon one's attitude. I always think of the word *repent* when I see a road sign that reads "No U-turns." Repentance is the opposite of this sign because repentance requires a "U-turn." To truly repent means to turn around, to stop going in the direction you are going, and to go in the opposite direction.

*Now when they heard this, they were pricked in their
heart, and said unto Peter and to the rest of the apostles,
Men and brethren, what shall we do? Then Peter said
unto them, Repent, and be baptized every one of you in
the name of Jesus Christ for the remission of sins, and ye
shall receive the gift of the Holy Ghost. For the promise
is unto you, and to your children, and to all that are
afar off, even as many as the Lord our God shall call.
And with many other words did he testify and exhort saying, Save yourselves from this untoward generation.
Then they that gladly received his word were baptized:
and the same day there were added unto them about
three thousand souls* (Acts 2:37-41).

This passage clearly shows the effect of the cross.
When men realized what they had done in crucifying Jesus, their hearts were broken. "And I," said Jesus, "if I be
lifted up from the earth, will draw all men unto Me" (Jn.
12:32). Every man had a hand in that crime.

One time a missionary told the story of Jesus while
ministering in an Indian village. After he taught, he
showed lantern slides, depicting the life of Christ, against
the whitewashed wall of a house. When the cross appeared on the wall, one man rose from the audience and
ran forward. "Come down from that cross, Son of God,"
he cried. "I, not you, should be hanging there." When
the essence of the cross is understood, the heart is
pierced.

Such an experience demands a reaction. "Repent,"
said Peter, "first and foremost." What does repentance
mean? The word originally meant an afterthought.
Often a second thought shows that the first thought was

wrong and so the word came to mean a change of mind. But if a man is honest, a change of mind demands a change of action. Repentance must involve both a change of mind and a change of action. A man may change his mind and come to see that his actions were wrong, but still be so much in love with his old ways that he refuses to abandon them. A man also could change his ways because of fear or coercion, but his mind may remain unchanged. True repentance involves both a change of mind and a change of action.

When repentance comes, something happens to the past. God's forgiveness covers what lies behind. Let me be clear, though; the consequences of sins are not wiped out. When we sin, we may well do something to ourselves and to others that cannot be undone. For example, when we were young and we did something bad, there was an invisible barrier between us and our mother. When we went and said we were sorry, the old relationship was restored and we were right with her again. Her acceptance of our apology does not abolish the consequences of what we did, but it puts us right with her. The same is true when we ask God's forgiveness. We are right with Him, but our past actions remain.

When repentance comes, something happens that affects the future. We receive the gift of the Holy Spirit and in that power we can win battles we never thought we could win. We can resist temptations that, by ourselves, we are powerless to resist.

C.S. Lewis said that repentance "is not something God demands of you before He will take you back...it is simply a description of what going back is like."

When Evangelist Gipsy Smith was preaching, he reminded his listeners that, if they truly received the Savior, their conduct would be revolutionized. He referred to this change of behavior as "stripe washing." Soon after the meeting, an elderly gentleman carrying a black satchel came to see him. He said he had been in the audience and was convicted about some money he had taken 40 years before. Recognizing that the man was deeply moved, the evangelist suggested that he should first get right with God and then straighten out matters with the people he had defrauded. As soon as he received Christ, the penitent one said, "Though it means traveling many miles, I'm going to return this money with interest to its rightful owner!" After restitution had been made, he exclaimed joyfully, "Now that I've been saved and have a clear conscience, I believe I'm truly the happiest man in the world!"

Day One

Part Three

The Church of the Called-Out Ones

Learning About Faith

The Greek word most commonly used in the New Testament for faith is *pistis* (pronounced: pis-tis). It is related to the word *peitho*, which means "to persuade." *Pistis* is a more intensive form of this word and primarily refers to a "firm persuasion." Persuasion, faith, or belief of this type emanates from conviction based upon hearing and is used in Matthew 8:10 and Acts 3:16 to describe faith in God, Christ, or things spiritual.

It also carries the meaning of (a) trust; (b) trustworthiness; (c) the contents of belief, which is a part of trust or faith; (d) a ground for "faith," an assurance; and (e) a pledge of fidelity. The main elements in "faith," in its relation to the invisible God, as distinct from "faith" in man, are especially brought out in the use of this noun and the corresponding verb, *pisteuo*. The variety of meanings for this concept of faith are (a) a firm conviction, producing a full acknowledgment of God's revelation or truth; (b) a personal surrender to Him; and (c) a conduct inspired by such surrender.

Prominence is given to one of these elements according to the context. All this stands in contrast to belief in its purely natural exercise, which consists of an opinion held in good "faith" without necessary reference to its proof. The object of Abraham's "faith" points to the way God initiates and makes covenants with His chosen people and pledges His love and faithfulness to them. In turn He demands their promise to reciprocate these same qualities toward Him. The evidence for faithfulness requires a sacrifice as the substitution of life for life. It gives us the first hint of God's provision for redemption from the forces of evil (compare Genesis 3:15 with Romans 16:17-20). It also contains the oldest and most profound definition of faith (see Gen. 15:6). The latter part of Hebrews chapter 11—a virtual roll call of the biblical faithful—refers to characters in Genesis.

Faith is a combination of three words: belief, acceptance, and trust. Grouped together, these words create the definition of faith. When one becomes a Christian, he must believe in Jesus Christ; he must accept Jesus Christ as his personal Savior; and he must trust Jesus Christ alone. This belief, acceptance, and trust forms the foundation of the Christian's confidence in Jesus and in His power to fulfill God's promise of salvation.

In its simplest form, faith means loyalty. When Paul wrote to the Thessalonians, he wished to know about their faith. In essence he was asking about their loyalty and how it was standing the test. In Second Thessalonians 1:4 faith and steadfastness are combined. Faith is the enduring fidelity that marks the real soldier of Jesus Christ.

Faith also can mean belief. In that situation it refers to the conviction that something is true. In First Corinthians 15:17 Paul tells the Corinthians that if Jesus did not rise from the dead, then their faith is vain; all that they have believed is wrecked. Thus faith confirms that the Christian message is true.

Faith sometimes is used as a substitute word for describing the Christian religion (the faith). In Second Corinthians 13:5 Paul tells his opponents to examine themselves to see if they are holding to their faith; that is, to see if they are still within the Christian religion.

At times, faith may be the practical equivalent to indestructible hope. "For we walk," writes Paul, "by faith, not by sight" (2 Cor. 5:7).

Finally, the most characteristic Pauline use of faith is to refer to total acceptance and absolute trust. He likens it to "betting your life there is a one true God." Faith means being utterly sure that what Jesus said is true, and staking all time and eternity on that assurance. "I believe in God," said Stevenson, "and if I woke up in hell, I would still believe in him."

Learning About Sanctification

The Greek word *hagaiosune* (pronounced: hagi-o-suney) is translated "sanctification" in Second Thessalonians 2:13 and is used in two ways in the New Testament: (a) as one set apart to God, and (b) as the course of life befitting those so separated. Sanctification is the process through which one, through faith in Christ, enters into relationship with God.

Sanctification is also used in the New Testament to describe the separation of the believer from evil things and ways. Sanctification is God's will for the believer and is the purpose behind the gospel message. The process through which one becomes sanctified is a process that can only be learned through God's revelation and His Word. The believer is exhorted to pursue the sanctified life earnestly and without deviation.

To be sanctified is to be holy. Both of these English words come from the same Greek word, *hagiosune*. Holiness is not vicarious, so it cannot be transferred or imputed. It is an individual possession, built up little by little, through obedience to the Word of God and by following the example of Christ with the help and power of the Holy Spirit. The Holy Spirit is the Agent in the process of sanctification (see Rom. 15:16; 2 Thess. 2:13; 1 Pet. 1:2).

In Vine's *Dictionary of New Testament Words*[1], sanctification by the Spirit is associated with the choice or election of God. It is a divine act preceding the acceptance of the gospel by the individual.

In the Old Testament, "things" were sanctified unto God. In this sense, the word literally means to "set apart for the service of God." Throughout the Old Testament, God continuously set aside things for His service. The "fire" that burned on the altar was sanctified, as was the

---

1.   Nashville, TN: Thomas Nelson Publishers, 1985.

ark that carried the scrolls of the covenant. The cup that Belshazzar defiled was sanctified (see Dan. 5).

The pagan world was lawless in that men's lusts were their only flaws. Lust, which violated the law, produced more lawlessness. This is true of man's sinful nature too. Sin begets sin. The first time you do a sinful thing, you may hesitate as a feeling of guilt or fear comes over you. The second time is easier and the more sin is practiced, the more desensitized you become. Before long, the sinful act becomes routine and is embraced without considering the right or wrong of it. Finally, all the thrills that sin produces cannot be satisfied with an occasional indulgence. The time comes when you need more and more of it to produce the same thrills. Sin left unchecked leads to more sin; lawlessness produces lawlessness.

In the New Testament, we find people who are being sanctified. The new life in Christ is different. It is a life grounded in righteous deeds. The Greeks defined righteousness as giving to man and to God their due. A Christian life, which flows from the righteousness of Jesus, is one that gives God His proper place and that respects the rights of human personality. The Christian will never disobey God nor ever use a human being to gratify his desire for pleasure.

The Greek word *hagiasmos* (sanctification) implies a process in progress, one that is not yet complete. The end of the road is holiness. When a man gives his life to Christ, he is not yet perfect. The struggle for perfection is by no means over. But Christianity has always regarded the direction a man is facing or travelling toward as more important than the particular stage he has reached. Once he is Christ's, he has started the process of sanctification and has embarked on the way or the road to holiness.

An old farmer frequently described his Christian experience by saying, "Well, I'm not making much progress, but I'm established!" One spring when he was hauling some logs, his wagon wheels sank down in mud up to the axles. Try as he would, he couldn't get the wagon out. Defeated, he sat atop the logs, surveying the dismal situation. Soon a neighbor, who had always felt uncomfortable with the farmer's worn-out testimony, came along and greeted him, "Well, Brother Jones, I see you're not making much progress, but you must be content because you're well established!" A Christian may be "established" in his sanctification, but if he is stuck in the mud he's not very productive. Too many of us are like that farmer.

Day One

Part Four

The Church Becoming the Body of Christ

In our first definition of the Christian church, we examined the various steps in the process of growth by each individual member of the community. The church community, as *ecclesia* (called-out ones), is governed by the New Testament, which is the perpetual and eternal constitution of the Church. When one enters the Church fellowship as a believer in Jesus Christ, he becomes a part of the family of God. The *ecclesia* represents the Kingdom of God in action, a kingdom that is within each member. As the Church is perpetual and eternal, so is the individual member a permanent resident of the Kingdom and a member of the Body of Christ.

The Community of the Redeemed

The second definition of the Church comes from the Greek word *koinonia* (pronounced: koin-o-ney-ah). This describes the Church as an organization or institution, a "community of the redeemed" as it functions. The launching of this *koinonia* (community) took place on the Day of Pentecost. Historically, it was the custom of the Jews to go to Jerusalem each year for this festival to give thanks for the harvest. The festival was widely attended and many people crowded the streets of Jerusalem in anticipation of the events associated with the festival. Acts 2:5 mentions that there were "devout men, out of every nation" who heard the apostles and disciples speaking in their own languages. After Peter spoke, it is apparent that many from this group believed the good news and entered into fellowship with the Jerusalem believers. Acts 2:41 tells us that about 3,000 were added to the community that day.

The Greek word *koinonia*, which describes this early Christian community, means "fellowship" or "partnership." Underlying this early meaning is the understanding that those who are in *koinonia* with one another share and have in common both beliefs and things. In the Christian sense today, it refers to members of an assembly or church on earth, saints in Heaven, or both.

The scene in Acts 2 begins with approximately 120 faithful followers assembled in an upper room near Jerusalem. They were together and in one accord, waiting as Jesus had instructed. They were also watching expectantly for divine revelation. They were not to be disappointed.

And when the day of Pentecost was fully come, they were all with one accord in one place. And suddenly there came a sound from heaven as of a rushing mighty wind, and it filled all the house where they were sitting.

And there appeared unto them cloven tongues like as of fire, and it sat upon each of them. And they were all filled with the Holy Ghost, and began to speak with other tongues, as the Spirit gave them utterance (Acts 2:1-4).

From that moment forward the Holy Spirit became the dominant reality in the life of the early Church. The Holy Spirit became the source of inspiration for their new life together as He assumed His position as Comforter and Guide. The Spirit moved Philip to make contact with the Ethiopian eunuch; prepared Peter for the coming of the emissaries of Cornelius; ordered Peter to go without hesitation with these emissaries; enabled Agabus to foretell the coming famine; ordered the setting apart of Paul and Barnabas for the momentous step of taking the gospel to the Gentiles; guided the decisions of the council of Jerusalem; guided Paul past Asia, Mysia, and Bithynia, down into Troas and then to Europe; and told Paul what awaited him in Jerusalem (see Acts 8:29; 10:19; 11:12,28; 13:2,4; 15:28; 16:6-8; 20:23). The early Church was a *koinonia*, a fellowship, a community guided by the Spirit of God.

The leaders of this new community were men filled with the Spirit. Of these leaders seven men "full of the Holy Ghost" were chosen for specific ministry (see Acts 6:3). Stephen and Barnabas are identified as men who were full of the Spirit (see Acts 7:55; 11:24). Paul tells the elders at Ephesus that it was the Spirit who made them overseers of the Church of God (see Acts 20:28).

The Holy Spirit was the source of day-to-day courage and power. The disciples received power when the Spirit came; Peter's courage and eloquence before the Sanhedrin resulted from the activity of the Spirit; and Paul's conquest of Elymas was the work of the Spirit (see Acts 1:8; 4:31; 13:9). The courage to meet a dangerous situation; the power to cope with life's obstacles; the eloquence to speak with authority; the joy, which is independent of circumstances—all of these qualities are ascribed to the work of the Spirit.

Finally, Acts 5:32 speaks of the Spirit "whom God hath given to them that obey Him." This verse contains a great truth and speaks of the need for a man to respond to God in order to receive all that God has to give. If a man is honestly trying to do the will of God, he will experience more and more of the wonder of the Spirit.

Then they that gladly received his word were baptized: and the same day there were added unto them about three thousand souls. And they continued stedfastly in the apostles' doctrine and fellowship, and in breaking of bread, and in prayers. And fear came upon every soul: and many wonders and signs were done by the apostles. And all that believed were together, and had all things common; and sold their possessions and goods, and parted them to all men, as every man had need. And they, continuing daily with one accord in the temple, and breaking bread from house to house, did eat their meat with gladness and singleness of heart, praising God, and having favour with all the people. And the Lord added to the church daily such as should be saved (Acts 2:41-47).

In this passage we have a summary of the characteristics of the early Church. These characteristics are broken down in the following list:

1. It was a learning Church and it persisted in listening to the apostles as they taught. One of the great perils of a church is to look back instead of forward. Because the riches of Christ are inexhaustible, we should ever be going forward. We should count a day wasted when we do not learn something new and when we have not penetrated more deeply into the wisdom and the grace of God.

2. It was a Church of fellowship and it had what someone has called "the great quality of togetherness." Admiral Nelson explained one of his victories by saying, "I had the happiness to command a band of brothers." The Church is the real Church only when it is a band of brothers.

3. It was a praying Church; these early Christians knew they could not meet life in their own strength. They also knew they did not need to rely on their own strength. They always went to God before they went out into the world. They were able to meet the problems of life because they had first met Him.

4. It was a reverent Church. In Acts 2:43 the word which the King James Version translates "fear" can best be understood to mean "awe." It was said of a great Greek leader that he moved through this world as if it were a temple. The Christian lives in reverence because he knows that the whole earth is the temple of the living God.

5. It was a Church where things happened, where signs and wonders were evident (see Acts 2:43). If we expect great things from God and attempt great things for God, then great things will happen. More things would happen if we believed that God, through us, could make them happen.

6. It was a sharing Church (see Acts 2:44-45). These early Christians had an intense feeling of responsibility for each other. It was said of William Morris that he never saw a drunken man without feeling a personal responsibility for him. A real Christian cannot bear to have too much when others have too little.

7. It was a worshiping Church (see Acts 2:46). They never forgot to visit God's house. We must remember, "God knows nothing of solitary religion." Things can happen when we come together because God's Spirit moves upon His worshiping people.

8. It was a happy Church (see Acts 2:46). The early Church was filled with gladness. A gloomy Christian is a contradiction in terms.

9. It was a Church that others could not help liking. There are two Greek words for good. *Agathos* simply describes a thing as good. *Kalos* means that a thing is not only good, but it also looks good. Real Christianity is a lovely thing. There are so many people who are good, but with their goodness possess a streak of hardness. In the early Church there was a sense of caring and compassion that was reflected in each person's appearance.

Establishing the Organization

The Church as a group became the institutional Church. It functioned as an independent community within a community. It was a community consisting of redeemed people. Thus the New Testament *koinonia* literally means "a community of the redeemed."

The organization of the Church was simple. Initially there were only two classes in the institutional Church. These classes were made up of apostles and converts (preachers and members). Their method of financing the church work was to establish a common treasury. Each member would "sell all that he had" and put the results of the sale in the common treasury.

> *Neither was there any among them that lacked: For as many as were possessors of lands or houses sold them, and brought the prices of the things that were sold, and laid them down at the apostles' feet: and distribution was made unto every man according as he had need* (Acts 4:34-35).

The apostles began to serve as the finance committee, which increased their responsibilities. They undertook the task of providing for the needs of the community out of the proceeds of the common treasury. Jesus had assigned them the "work of the Church." The Church placed upon them "church work." This arrangement was simplistic and commendable, but built into it were the seeds of destruction. These seeds sprouted within a few weeks and the Church experienced its first "church fight."

> *And in those days, when the number of the disciples was multiplied, there arose a murmuring of the Grecians against the Hebrews, because their widows were neglected in the daily ministration. Then the twelve called the multitude of the disciples unto them, and said, It is not reason that we should leave the word of God, and serve tables. Wherefore, brethren, look ye out among you seven men of honest report, full of the Holy Ghost and*

wisdom, whom we may appoint over this business (Acts 6:1-3).

The solution was to share the responsibility with representatives from the community itself. The qualifications were quite simple:

1.   Be a person of honest report;
2.   Be filled of the Holy Ghost;
3.   Demonstrate godly wisdom.

(As a pastor I think the apostles should have added another prerequisite: They *should be available.*) This group, called "deacons," were assigned the task of dealing with conflict in the Church. A deacon's link with the pastor can be a blessing to any church. Thus pastors and deacons ought to have unbreakable bonds in Jesus Christ.

Day One Summary

This is the Church defined and applied. The Church "within" is the first step in establishing the Church of the Lord Jesus Christ. The Church "without" is the second step in establishing the Church's doing the work ordained by Jesus Christ. This means the Church must be in a person before that person is in the Church. As a member of the Body of Christ, you are called to reside in the Kingdom and to be an ambassador for the Kingdom. As you live your life as a productive member of Christ's community, live it in the joy and power of the Holy Spirit. You will be a credit and a blessing to yourself, to your family, and to your community, and you will bring glory to God.

Day Two

Part One

The Emerging Ministry

Now that we have defined the Church as the *Ecclesia* (the Church within) and the *Koinonia* (the Church without), and we have seen the way in which the officers were selected in Acts 6, we must now turn to the issue of ministry. Specifically, we need to consider the role of the minister to complete the organization.

In our seminar format we ask the participants to help us define the characteristics of a good minister. Usually this is done aloud so all can feel free to participate. I encourage you to stop reading and, right now, take a couple of minutes to write down a list of characteristics you consider essential for a good minister.

Now that you have your list in hand, look at these two verses from Paul's letter to the Ephesians:

And He gave some, apostles; and some, prophets; and some, evangelists; and some, pastors and teachers; for the perfecting of the saints, for the work of the ministry, for the edifying of the body of Christ (Ephesians 4:11-12).

I would like to place an emphasis on the words "the work of the ministry." God gives ministry gifts to the Church so the saints (members) may be perfected (grow to maturity) for the work of the ministry. God's purpose is to bring maturity to the lives of the members so they can do the work of edifying (building up) the Body of Christ, which is the Church. Members of the Church are responsible for doing the work of the ministry and are thus called "ministers of the Church."

Therefore, every member of the Church is a potential minister. This is the result of God's giving the Church ministry gifts (apostles, prophets, evangelists, pastors, and teachers) to help them grow to maturity.

Defining the Characteristics of a Minister

For ministers (members) of the Church, there are essential qualities or characteristics necessary to lead others into maturity and thereby build up the "Body of Christ." Those who have the peculiar responsibility of extending the ministry of the Church must have experience and a resolute commitment.

A. A Minister of the Church Must Be Holy

We have studied the Greek word for sanctification, *hagaiosune*, and we now are faced with a similar word, *hagiasmos* (pronounced: hag-ee-as-mos'), which means "holiness." As we mentioned before, these two words, *sanctification* and *holiness*, are two aspects of the same thing.

Hagiasmos in the Revised Standard Version is usually translated "sanctification." It signifies three things.

1. It is used in Romans 1:4 of the absolute "holiness" of Christ during His days in the flesh. This is the characteristic that distinguished Him from all other human beings. The absolute holiness of Jesus, which is indicated in the phrase "the spirit of holiness," along with His resurrection from the dead, established Him as the Son of God.

2. According to Second Corinthians 7:1, believers are to be "perfecting holiness in the fear of God" and bringing "holiness" to its predestined end.

3. The end is that they may be found "unblamable in holiness" in the *parousia* (coming again) of Christ.

There is often confusion when someone uses the word *holy*. It carries with it the preconceived notion that someone is being exalted beyond merit. You are no doubt familiar with the sarcastic use of the phrase "holier than thou." The classic image of a holy person is one who is dressed in black and goes about with a somber attitude. The paradigm is a Bible-toting, Scripture-quoting, angelic-faced person who is above the affairs of the world. Nothing could be farther from the truth. Paul speaks of holiness in Romans 12: "I beseech you therefore, brethren, by the mercies of God, that ye present your bodies a living sacrifice, holy, acceptable unto God, which is your reasonable service" (Rom 12:1).

There are a number of mental obstacles to understanding holiness. If we can set these aside, we will go a long way toward accepting the charge "be ye holy, for I am holy" (1 Pet. 1:16).

1. Holiness has an ominous ring to it. It suggests a life style that is impossible to reach. It tends to discourage new converts from trying. Holiness, like perfection, when left unexplained, tends to be counterproductive.

2. Holiness is associated with struggle and suffering. The standard church hymns promise a life of strain and struggle. One cannot look forward to Christian commitment when the future promises "trial dark on every hand, that we cannot understand. Our hearts are made to bleed for some thoughtless word or deed. We wonder why the test when we try to do our best, but we will understand it better by and by."

3. Holiness suggests a propensity to judge, often to the extreme. It appears to "beat up" on people, and show the superiority of Christians. Non-Christians, who are the target of our missionary endeavors, shun Christians because they fear they will be judged harshly.

Paul's statement in Romans 12:1 seems very clear to me. Presenting our bodies a living sacrifice is a matter of giving God service that is within reason. The next verse, Romans 12:2, is truly a revelation or expansion of the meaning of the first verse. "And be not conformed to this world: but be ye transformed by the renewing of your mind...." Holiness deals with service and acceptable service has to be done with the right attitude.

We are judged by the attitude we demonstrate in our relationships with one another. A proper attitude will refrain from judgmental behavior and seek a common bond with our fellow laborers in the gospel. Paul, in a sense, was applying Jesus' answer concerning the greatest commandment in a practical way.

Jesus said unto him, Thou shalt love the Lord thy God with all thy heart, and with all thy soul, and with all thy mind. This is the first and great commandment. And the second is like unto it, Thou shalt love thy neighbor as thyself. On these two commandments hang all the law and the prophets (Matthew 22:37-40).

Paul's paraphrasing of these commandments stated the same laws in reverse. One must love himself, in order to love his neighbor, in order to love God.

Holiness is a characteristic unique to God's nature that becomes the goal for human morality. The idea of "holy" is important for an understanding of God, of worship, and of the people of God in the Bible. "Holy" has three distinct meanings.

1. To be holy means to be "set apart." This applies to places where God is present, like the temple and the tabernacle, and to things and people related to those holy places or to God Himself.

2. It means to be "perfect, transcendent, or spiritually pure, evoking adoration and reverence." This applies primarily to God, but secondarily to saints or godly people.

3. It means something or someone who evokes "veneration or awe, being frightening beyond belief." This is clearly applied to God and is the primary meaning of "holy." It is continued in the last definition: "filled with superhuman and potentially fatal power." This speaks of God, but also of places, things, or people who have been set apart by God's calling or presence. A saint is a holy person. To be sanctified is to be made holy.

In the Old Testament, "holy" is important as it relates to the priesthood and worship. The Book of Leviticus, especially chapter 16, deals with these subjects. It is also found throughout the prophetic books of the Old Testament. Isaiah's title for God is "the Holy One of Israel" and he describes the adoration of God by the seraphim in Isaiah chapter 6. The word is also found repeatedly in the Book of Psalms. Holiness is showing an interest in others through loving, caring, and sharing. Personal, one-on-one evangelism is establishing a loving relationship with people in order to lead them to Christ. The act of being holy is not what we say, but what we do.

One day John Wesley was preaching at an open-air meeting in the slums of London. Many people had gathered to hear him speak. At the back of the crowd stood two ruffians who were intent on disrupting the meeting. One said to the other, "Who is this preacher? What right does he have to come here and tell us how to live?" Picking up stones, they moved forward until they got very close to Wesley. As he talked about Christ's power to change men's lives, he was so filled with the love of God that a warmth and beauty spread over his countenance. The two hecklers stopped short and were dumbfounded as they saw his radiant face. With a note of awe in his voice one of them said, "He ain't a man, Bill; he ain't a man!" The stones fell from their hands and their hearts were softened as they listened. When Wesley finished and began to leave, he saw the two ruffians. Putting his hands on their shoulders, he said, "God bless you, my boys," and continued on his way. As he disappeared into the crowd, one of the fellows exclaimed, "He *is* a man, Bill; he *is* a man, but he's a man like God!"

Rules to Live By

Paul presents the churches he writes to with ten rules for ordinary, everyday life. Let us look at them one by one.

1. Love must be completely sincere. There must be no hypocrisy, no play-acting, and no ulterior motive. There is such a thing as cupboard love, which gives affection with one eye on the gain that may result. There is such a thing as selfish love; its aim is to get far more than it is to give. Christian love is cleansed of self; it is a pure outpouring of the heart to others.

2. We must hate that which is evil and cling to that which is good. It has been said that our one security against sin lies in our being shocked by it. It was Carlyle who said that what we need is to see the infinite beauty of holiness and the infinite damnability of sin. It has been said that no virtue is safe that is not passionate. We must hate evil and love good. Regarding one thing, we must be clear: What many people hate is not evil, but the consequences of evil. No man is really a good man when he is good simply because he fears the consequences of being bad. Not to fear the consequences of dishonor, but to love honor passionately, is the way to real goodness.

3. We must be affectionate to one another in brotherly love. The Greek word Paul uses for affectionate is *philostorgos*. *Storge* is the Greek word for family love. We must love each other because we are members of one family. We are not strangers to each other within the Christian church, much less isolated units. We are brothers and sisters because we all have one Father, who is God.

4. We must give each other priority in honor. More than half the trouble that arises in churches concerns rights, privileges, and prestige. Someone has not been given his place, or someone has been neglected or unappreciated. The mark of the true Christian has always been humility.

One of the humblest of men was that great saint and scholar Principal Cairns. Someone recorded an incident which showed Cairns as he was. He was a guest on the platform at a great gathering. As he appeared there was a tremendous burst of applause. Cairns stood back to let the man next to him pass and he began to applaud himself. He never dreamed that the applause was for him.[1]

It is not easy to give each other priority in honor. There is enough of the natural man in most of us to cause us to demand our rights, but the Christian man has no rights—he has only duties.

5. We must not be sluggish in zeal. There is a certain intensity in the Christian life; there is no room for lethargy in it. The Christian cannot take things in an easygoing way because the world is a battleground between good and evil. The time is short, and life is a preparation for eternity. The Christian may burn out, but he must not rust out.

6. We must keep our spirits at the boiling point. The one man whom the risen Christ could not stand was the man who was neither hot nor cold (see Rev. 3:15-16). Today people are apt to look askance upon enthusiasm.

1. *Sermon Illustrations for Windows,* by NAVPRESS, P.O. Box 6000, Colorado Springs, CO 80934. Used by permission.

The modern battle cry is, "I couldn't care less." The Christian, however, is a man desperately earnest. He is on fire for Christ.

7. Paul's seventh injunction may be one of two things. The ancient manuscripts offer two readings. Some read "serve the Lord" and some read "serve the time," which means "grasp your opportunities." The reason for the double reading is that all the ancient Christian scribes used contractions in their writing. In particular, the more common words were sometimes abbreviated. One of the most common ways of abbreviating was to leave out the vowels, as shorthand does, and to place a stroke along the top of the remaining letters. For example, the word for Lord is *kurios* and the word for time is *kairos*. The abbreviation for both of these words is *krs*. In these verses, filled with practical advice, it is more likely that Paul was saying to his people, "Seize your opportunities as they come."

Life presents us with a variety of opportunities: the opportunity to learn something new or to avoid something wrong; the opportunity to speak a word of encouragement or of a word of warning; or the opportunity to help or to comfort. One of the tragedies of life is that we so often fail to grasp these opportunities when they present themselves. There are three things which do not come back: the spent arrow, the spoken word, and the lost opportunity.

8. We are to rejoice in hope. When Alexander the Great was setting out on one of his eastern campaigns, he distributed all kinds of gifts to his friends. In his generosity he had given away nearly all his possessions. "Sir,"

said one of his friends, "you will have nothing left for yourself." "Oh, yes, I have," said Alexander, "I still have my hopes." The Christian must be an optimist. Because God is God, the Christian is always certain that "the best is yet to be." Because he knows of the grace that is sufficient for all things and the strength that is made perfect in weakness, the Christian knows that no task is too much for him. There are no hopeless situations in life; there are only men who have grown hopeless about them. There can never be any such thing as a hopeless Christian.

9. We are to meet tribulation with triumphant fortitude. Someone once said to a gallant sufferer: "Suffering colors all life, doesn't it?" "Yes," said the gallant one, "it does, but I propose to choose the color." When the dreadful affliction of complete deafness began to descend on Beethoven and life seemed to be one unbroken disaster, he said, "I will take life by the throat." As William Cowper put it:

> Set free from present sorrow,
> We cheerfully can say,
> Even let the unknown tomorrow,
> Bring with it what it may,
> It can bring with it nothing,
> But he will bear us through.

When Nebuchadnezzar cast Shadrach, Meshach, and Abednego into the fiery furnace, he was amazed that they suffered no harm. He asked if three men had not been cast into the flames. They told him it was so. He said, "Lo, I see four men loose, walking in the midst of the fire, and they have no hurt; and the form of the fourth is like the Son of God" (Dan. 3:25). A man can endure anything when he goes through it with Christ.

10. We are to persevere in prayer. Is it not the case that there are times in life when we let day add itself to day and week to week, and we never speak to God? When a man ceases to pray, he despoils himself of the strength of Almighty God. No man should be surprised when life collapses if he insists on living it alone.

B. A Minister Must Be Steadfast

The Greek word *hedraios* (pronounced: he-rah'-yos) is a derivative from the Greek word *hezomai* meaning "to sit." The implication is one that leads us to understand that steadfastness is something placed in such a way that it is immovable. *Hedraios* primarily refers to being "seated" or "settled." The word is extended to mean "a support, foundation," and denotes "strength, steadfastness." It is used of the firmament, which was believed to be a solid canopy. The corresponding Hebrew word *raqia* means "expanse," from *raqa*, "to spread out."

Steadfastness should be understood to mean "to endure patiently." A steadfast person is one who is reliable, faithful, and true to the end. Paul said that Jesus was a person of steadfastness (see Rom. 15:3-4). The New International Version translates steadfastness as "perseverance" (see 2 Thess. 1:4). James said that trials that test our faith produce steadfastness, patience, endurance, and perseverance (see Jas. 1:3).

Wherefore seeing we also are compassed about with so great a cloud of witnesses, let us lay aside every weight, and the sin which doth so easily beset us, and let us run

with patience the race that is set before us, looking unto
Jesus the author and finisher of our faith; who for the joy
that was set before Him endured the cross, despising the
shame, and is set down at the right hand of the throne of
God (Hebrews 12:1-2).

This is one of the great, moving passages of the New
Testament, and the writer has given us an almost perfect
summary of the Christian life. The elements of this verse
include the following:

1. In the Christian life we have a goal. The Christian
is not an unconcerned stroller along the byways of life;
he is a wayfarer on the high road. He is not a tourist who
returns each night to the place from which he starts; he
is a pilgrim who is forever on the way. The goal is nothing less than the likeness of Christ. The Christian life is
going somewhere, and it would be well if, at each day's
ending, we were to ask ourselves: "Am I any farther
down the path?"

2. In the Christian life we have an inspiration. We
have the thought of the unseen cloud of witnesses. They
are witnesses in a double sense. They have witnessed
their confession to Christ and they are now witnesses of
our performance. The Christian is like a runner in some
crowded stadium. As he presses on, the crowd looks
down and the people in the crowd are those who have already won the crown.

An actor would act with double intensity if he knew
that a group of Academy Award-winning actors were sitting in the audience watching him. A basketball player
would strive with double effort if he knew that Michael
Jordan, Magic Johnson, and Doctor "J" were watching

him. It is the very essence of the Christian life that it is lived in the gaze of the heroes of the faith who lived, suffered, and died in their day. How can a man avoid the struggle for greatness with an audience like that looking down upon him?

3. In the Christian life we have a handicap. If we are encircled by the greatness of the past, we are also encircled by the handicap of our own sin. No man would seek to climb Mount Everest with a load of lumber weighing him down. If we would travel far, we must travel light. There is, in life, an essential duty of discarding things. There may be habits, pleasures, self-indulgences, or associations that hold us back. We must shed them as an athlete sheds his track suit when he goes to the starting mark. Often we will need the help of Christ to enable us to do so.

4. In the Christian life we have a means. That means is steadfast endurance. That word does not mean the patience that sits down and accepts things, but the patience that masters them. It is not some romantic thing that lends us wings to fly over the difficulties and the hard places. It is a steady, unhurried determination that goes on and refuses to be deflected. Obstacles do not daunt such determination and discouragements do not take away hope. It is the steadfast endurance that carries on until, in the end, it achieves the goal set before it.

5. In the Christian life we have an example. That example is Jesus Himself. For the goal that was set before Him, He endured all things. To win the battle meant to walk the way of the cross. The writer to the Hebrews had a blast of insight when he said that Jesus despised the

shame. Jesus was sensitive; never had any person so sensitive a heart as He. A cross was a humiliating thing. It was for criminals, for those whom society regarded as the dregs of humanity, and yet he accepted the responsibility. St. Philip of Neri bids us "to despise the world, to despise ourselves, and to despise—the fact that we are despised." If Jesus could endure like that, so must we.

6. In the Christian life we have a presence. It is the presence of Jesus. He is at once the goal of our journey and our companion along the way; at once the One whom we go to meet and the One with whom we travel. The wonder of the Christian life is that we press on surrounded by the saints, oblivious to everything but the glory of the goal. We are forever in the company of Him who has already made the journey and reached the goal, and who waits to welcome us when we reach the end.

The expression "stood fixed" comes from a practice dating back to the great architecture of many years ago. It means "without wax." The builders would build great buildings out of marble. When the building was completed it had to undergo rigid inspection. The less honorable builders would seal the imperfect joints with wax, then paint over the waxed joints. When the temperature reached 110 degrees, the wax would melt and expose the faulty joints. To be steadfast is to be without fault in your pursuit of your goal.

Day Two

Part Two

The Role of the Holy Spirit in Ministry

A new debate and controversy about the Holy Spirit has arisen lately. But whatever may be the discussion about methods, manners, and procedures as related to the Holy Spirit, we can agree that the Holy Spirit works in three distinct experiences: the receiving of the Holy Spirit, the filling of the Holy Spirit, and the baptism of the Holy Spirit.

A. A Minister Must Receive the Holy Spirit

The Greek word *pneuma* (pronounced: noo-mah) means "a current of air, breath (blast) or a breeze." By analogy or figuratively, it also means a "spirit." This can refer to the rational soul (which contains the will, the emotions, and the intellect) or superhuman beings, such as an angel or a demon. It also may be used when referring to divine beings, angels of God, and Christ's Spirit, whom we call the Holy Spirit or Holy Ghost.

✴ The believer receives the indwelling of the Holy Spirit the moment that Jesus Christ is accepted as one's personal Savior.

But ye are not in the flesh, but in the Spirit, if so be that the Spirit of God dwell in you. Now if any man have not the Spirit of Christ, he is none of His (Romans 8:9).

If ye love Me, keep My commandments. And I will pray the Father, and He shall give you another Comforter, that He may abide with you for ever; even the Spirit of truth; whom the world cannot receive, because it seeth Him not, neither knoweth Him: but ye know Him; for He dwelleth with you, and shall be in you (John 14:15-17).

Jesus does not leave us to struggle with the Christian life alone. He promised to send us a Helper. The Greek word for this Helper is *parakletos,* which is hard to translate with a single word. The King James Version renders it Comforter, which although hallowed by time and usage, is not a good translation. Moffatt translates it as Helper. It is only when we examine this word *parakletos* in detail that we catch something of the riches of the doctrine of the Holy Spirit. It really means someone who is called or sent to assist another. Certain subtleties are attached to the word based on the reason the *parakletos* is called.

The Greeks used the word in a variety of ways. A *parakletos* might be a person called in to give witness in a law court on behalf of a defendant; he might be an advocate called in to plead the cause of someone under a charge that might result in a serious penalty; or he might be an expert called in to give advice in some difficult situation. He might be a person called in when, for example, a company of soldiers were depressed and dispirited. In this last instance the *parakletos* would instill new courage into their minds and hearts. Always a *parakletos* is someone called in to help in time of trouble or need. In this sense, "comforter" may be considered a perfectly good translation. It actually goes back to Wycliffe, the first translator to use it. But in his day it meant much more than it means now. The Latin word *fortis*, which was used to translate the Greek *parakletos*, means brave. A comforter was someone who enabled some dispirited creature to be brave.

Nowadays comfort has to do almost solely with sorrow; thus a comforter is someone who sympathizes with us when we are sad. Beyond a doubt the Holy Spirit does that, but to limit His work to that function is sadly to belittle Him. We often talk of being able to cope with things. That is precisely the work of the Holy Spirit. He takes away our inadequacies and enables us to cope with life. The Holy Spirit substitutes victorious living for defeated living.

B. A Minister Must Be Filled With the Holy Ghost

The Spirit of the Lord is upon Me, because He hath anointed Me to preach the gospel to the poor; He hath sent Me to heal the brokenhearted, to preach deliverance to the captives, and recovering of sight to the blind, to set at liberty them that are bruised, to preach the acceptable year of the Lord (Luke 4:18-19).

To be filled with the Holy Spirit for ministry is to be committed to the five classes of people whom Jesus identified and came to minister unto:

1. the poor;

2. the brokenhearted;

3. the captives;

4. the blind;

5. the bruised.

Earlier we observed Paul's statement that holiness is related to service. (See Romans 12:1 concerning "reasonable service.") Immediately after Jesus' temptation in the wilderness, He tells us what it means to be filled with the Holy Spirit.

The Spirit of the Lord is upon Me, because He hath anointed Me to preach the gospel to the poor; He hath sent Me to heal the brokenhearted, to preach deliverance to the captives, and recovering of sight to the blind, to set at liberty them that are bruised, to preach the acceptable year of the Lord (Luke 4:18-19).

This passage tells of the Messiah's ministry of preaching and healing—to meet every human. He was anointed for this purpose, not with literal oil (see Ex. 30:22-31), but with the Holy Spirit. "...This day is this scripture fulfilled in your ears" (Lk. 4:21). A summary of this passage may well serve as a guide for all preaching. The basic form or elements would be to present the teaching of Holy Scripture, drawing it together in one sentence, and to focus the sentence as to substance. He applies this in the good news He proclaims to the poor, the release which He announces to the captives, the healing which He offers to those whom sin has blinded, and the freedom He brings to those who are bruised.

This was not what the religious leaders expected. Neither was this the word of redemption they expected. They had wanted a word to raise carnal hopes, to flatter

Jewish pride. Truly, it was a most un-Jewish discourse for a Jewish Messiah. Yet the power of these "words of grace" was such that the hearers were spellbound by His announcement. Every eye was fastened on Him with hunger and eagerness. For the time they forgot all else. Even the strangeness of the message, in stark contrast to the preaching of teachers in their synagogue, was forgotten. In this setting Jesus' words walked up and down on the hearts of men.

Indeed, one can scarcely conceive the impression the words of Christ must have produced. Words filled with promise, hope, and reality offered to satiate the desires of the heart long left unfilled. These desires were now awakened again and at the same time satisfied. Truly the anointing of the Holy Spirit was on the Preacher, whose lips offered these "words of grace." The proclamation went forth that this was "the acceptable year of the Lord."

Cecil Northcott in *A Modern Epiphany* tells of a discussion in a camp of young people where representatives of many nations were living together. "One wet night the campers were discussing various ways of telling people about Christ. They turned to the girl from Africa. 'Maria,' they asked, 'what do you do in your country?' 'Oh,' said Maria, 'we don't have missions or give pamphlets away. We just send one or two Christian families to live and work in a village, and when people see what Christians are like, then they want to be Christians too.' " In the end the only all-conquering argument is the argument of a Christian life.[1]

---

1.   From *Dynamic Preaching*, a Publication of Seven Worlds Corporation, P.O. Box 11565, Knoxville, TN 37939. Used by permission.

C. The Baptism of the Holy Ghost

The subject of the baptism of the Holy Spirit is an extensive subject in itself, one with as many interpretations as there are theologies. Suffice it to say that it is a "special anointing, for a special person, with a special assignment, at a special time."

Day Two

Part Three

Ministry According to the Law of Love

A. A Minister Must Live By the Law of Love

The Greek word *agape* (pronounced: ag-ah'-pay) means love in the sense of affection or benevolence and even charity. *Agape* is used in the New Testament:

1. To describe the attitude of God toward His Son (see Jn. 17:26); toward the human race, generally (see Jn. 3:16; Rom. 5:8); and, toward such as believe on the Lord Jesus Christ, particularly (see Jn. 14:21);
2. To convey His will to His children concerning their attitude toward another (see Jn. 13:34) and toward all men (see 1 Cor. 16:14; 1 Thess. 3:12; 2 Pet. 1:7);
3. To express the essential nature of God (see 1 Jn. 4:8).

There are a number of passages that deal with the application of *agape* love, but none expresses it so succinctly as John 13:35: "By this shall all men know that ye are My disciples, if ye have love one to another."

When Jesus spoke these parting words to His disciples, He was leaving them with an important final instruction. The time was short and if they were ever to hear His voice, they must hear it now. He was going on a journey that He alone could take. He was taking a road He was predestined to travel and before He departed, He gave them this commandment to love one another as He had loved them. What does this mean to us and our relationships with our fellow men? How did Jesus love His disciples?

1. He loved his disciples selflessly. Even in human love there remains some element of self. We so often think, maybe unconsciously, of what we are to get in return. We think of the happiness we will receive, or of the loneliness we will suffer if love fails or is denied. So often we are thinking, "What will this love do for me?" So often at the back of love we seek happiness. But Jesus never thought of Himself. His one desire was to give Himself and all He had for those He loved.

2. Jesus loved His disciples sacrificially. There was no limit to His love. No demand could be placed on His love that was more than He was willing to offer. If love meant the cross, Jesus was prepared to go there. Sometimes we make the mistake of thinking that love is meant to give us happiness. Often, in the end, it does, but love may well bring pain and demand a cross.

3. Jesus loved His disciples and understood their strengths and their weaknesses. He knew His disciples

through and through. We never really know people until we have lived with them. When we meet someone occasionally, we see them at their best. It is when we live with them that we find out their moods, their weaknesses, and the things that irritate them. Jesus had lived with His disciples day in and day out for many months and knew all that was to know about them—and He still loved them.

Sometimes we say that love is blind. That is not so, for the love that is blind can end in nothing but bleak and utter disillusionment. Real love is open-eyed. It loves, not what it imagines a man to be, but who he is. The heart of Jesus is big enough to love us as we are.

4. Jesus loved His disciples with forgiveness. Peter would deny Him. All would forsake Him in His hour of need. While He was with them, they never really understood Him. They were blind and insensitive, slow to learn, and lacked understanding. In the end they were craven cowards. But Jesus held nothing against them. There was no failure that He would not forgive. Love that has not learned to forgive can do nothing else but shrivel and die. We are poor creatures and there is a kind of fate in things that makes us hurt those who love us best. For that very reason all enduring love must be built on forgiveness. Without forgiveness, love is bound to die.

If we are to be the kind of ministers that God wants and deserves, our ministry must offer a love that is selfless, sacrificial, understanding, and forgiving. John's letters to the Church places strong emphasis on love.

We know that we have passed from death unto life, because we love the brethren. He that loveth not his brother

abideth in death. Whosoever hateth his brother is a mur-
derer: and ye know that no murderer hath eternal life
abiding in him. Hereby perceive we the love of God, be-
cause He laid down His life for us: and we ought to lay
down our lives for the brethren (1 John 3:14-16).

John does more than move in the high realms of the-
ology. He has more practical things to say about the
Christian church and the Christian life. No New Testament writer stresses more consistently or more strenu-
ously the necessity of Christian fellowship. John was
convinced that Christians are not only bound to God,
they are also bound to each other. When we walk in the
light, we have fellowship with each other (see 1 Jn. 1:7).
The man who claims to walk in the light but hates his
brother, is in reality walking in darkness. It is the man
who loves his brother who is in the light (see 1 Jn. 2:9-11).
The proof that a man has passed from darkness to light
is the love he has for his brother. To hate one's brother
is, in essence, to be a murderer as Cain was. If any man,
out of his own supply, is able to help his brother who is
in poverty and does not do so, it is ridiculous for him to
claim that the love of God dwells in him. The essence of
religion is to believe on the name of the Lord Jesus
Christ and to love one another. God is love and, therefore, the man who loves is related to God. God has loved
us, and that is the best reason for loving each other (see
1 Jn. 4:7-12).

If a man says that he loves God and at the same time
hates his brother, he is a liar. The command is that he
who loves God must love his brother also (see 1 Jn. 4:20-21).
It was John's conviction that the only way a man can

prove that he loves God is by loving his fellow men. That love must be not only a sentimental emotion, but also a dynamic force ending in practical help.

Jesus' teaching of the greatest commandment, as recorded in Matthew, Mark, and Luke, restates the great proclamation of Israel recorded in Deuteronomy 6:4-5. The second greatest commandment, which Jesus said was like to the first, repeats Leviticus 19:18 ("Thou shalt love thy neighbour as thyself").

On one occasion a lawyer quoted the two commandments and then asked Jesus, "And who is my neighbour?" (Lk. 10:29). Jesus responded with the story of the Samaritan—the one who took care of the man who fell among robbers—to illustrate the selfless love that is to be characteristic of citizens of the Kingdom.

In Matthew 5:43-48, Jesus gave the radical command to love one's enemies and to pray for those who persecute you. Loving only those who love you is, according to Jesus, no better than how those who are not His disciples love others. The love that Jesus' disciples have for others is to be just as complete as God's love (see Mt. 5:48; compare Rom. 5:8).

Of course, in these teachings the selfless love called for is a response to God's prior activity. It is a way of life expected of those who are citizens of the Kingdom. The teachings of Jesus on loving our enemies, it will be noted, are a part of the Sermon on the Mount which is directed to Christian disciples (see Mt. 5).

In First Corinthians 13, Paul associated love with the all-important words of faith and hope (see also 1 Thess.

5:8; Gal. 5:6). Still, he declared love the greatest. The context for this passage on love is Paul's discussion of relationships in the Church. In First Corinthians 13:1-3 Paul indicates that the gifts of the Spirit (ecstatic speech, wisdom, faith, and self-sacrifice) without substance are without love. Love is the most important building block and with this in place, the Spirit distributes His gifts for the common good (see 1 Cor. 8:1; 12:7).

First Corinthians 13:4-7 characterizes love as patient and kind, not jealous or boastful, not arrogant or rude. Love is not selfish, irritable, or resentful. Love does not rejoice at wrong but in the right. Love bears, believes, hopes, and endures all things.

John uses one of Jesus' commandments in his first letter. He is putting a new twist on an old commandment. In First John 2:6 he says that he who abides in Jesus Christ must live the same kind of life as his Master lived. But almost certainly John is thinking of the words of Jesus: "A new commandment I give unto you, that ye love one another; as I have loved you, that ye also love one another" (Jn. 13:34). So in what sense was that commandment both old and new?

1. It was old in the sense that it was already evident in the Old Testament. Did not the law say, "Thou shalt love thy neighbour as thyself" (Lev. 19:18)? Many of the people to whom John was writing had heard this commandment many times before. But all who entered the Christian life had been taught that the law of love must be the law of their lives from the first day.

2. It was new in that it had been raised to a new standard in the life of Jesus. Jesus was making His own

love the example for those who followed after Him. They were to love each other as He had loved them. It could well be said that men did not really know what love was until they saw it in Him.

In every sphere of life it is possible for a thing to be old in the sense that it existed before, but then seem new because it was redefined by someone's use of it. A game may become a new game to a man when he has seen a real professional play it. A piece of music may become a new thing to a man when he has heard some great orchestra play it under the baton of a master conductor. Even a dish of food can become a new thing to a man after it has been prepared by someone with a genius for cooking. An old thing can become a new experience in the hands of a master. In Jesus, love became new in two directions.

1. It became new in that its reach was extended. In Jesus, love reached out to the sinner. To the orthodox rabbi, the sinner was a person whom God wished to destroy. "There is joy in heaven," they said, "when one sinner is obliterated from the earth."[1] But Jesus was the friend of outcast men and women and of sinners, and He was sure there was joy in Heaven when one sinner came home. In Jesus, love reached out to the Gentile. As the rabbis saw it, "The Gentiles were created by God to be fuel for the fires of Hell."[2]

But in Jesus "...God so loved the world, that He gave His only begotten Son" (see Jn. 3:16a). Love became new

---

1.   *The Bible Encyclopedia* (J. Mitchell Howard Co., 1901).
2.   Ibid.

in Jesus because He widened its boundaries until there were none outside its embrace.

2. It became new in the lengths to which it would go. No lack of response, nothing that men could ever do to Him, could turn Jesus' love to hate. He could even pray for God's mercy on those who were nailing Him to His cross.

In the final analysis, love, as applied to the Church and its ministry, is threefold. Love is an adventure, a dedication, and a sacrifice.

Love and Relationships

A. Love Is an Adventure Into a New Relationship

The missionary concept is built on searching out and establishing new relationships. Our marching orders are to venture into new territory, whether in Judea, Samaria, or the uttermost parts of the earth. This is what makes the *Ecclesia* (Church) feasible.

Jesus commissioned His disciples in Matthew 28 to go to all the nations. It was a command to venture into world relationships. He did three things in Matthew 28.

1. He gave them a commission. He sent them out to make all the nations His disciples. It may well be that the instruction to baptize is something that developed from the words of Jesus. That may be argued, but the fact remains that the commission of Jesus is to win all men for Himself.

2. He assured them of His power. Surely nothing was outside the power of Him who had died and conquered

death. Now they were the servants of a Master whose authority upon earth and in Heaven was beyond all question.

3. He promised them a presence. It must have been a staggering thing for 11 humble Galileans to be sent forth to conquer the world. Even as they heard it, their hearts must have failed them. But no sooner was the command given then the promise followed. They were sent out, as we are, on the greatest task in history. With them was the greatest presence in the world.

When God commissions us, He launches us upon a divine mission. He confers power upon us to perform a number of tasks.

1. The Church has a preaching task. It is the duty of the Church, and thus the duty of every Christian, to tell the story of the good news of Jesus to those who have never heard it. The Christian duty is to be the herald of Jesus.

2. The Church has a healing task. Here is a fact we have seen again and again. Christianity is concerned with men's bodies as well as men's minds. Jesus wished to bring health to the body and health to the soul.

3. The Church has a source of power. We need not take everything literally. We need not think that the Christian is literally to have the power to lift venomous snakes and drink poisonous liquids without harm. But at the back of this descriptive language is the conviction that the Christian is filled with a power to cope with life that others do not possess.

4. The Church is never left alone to do its work. Christ works with it, in it, and through it. The Lord of the Church is still in the Church and He is still the Lord or the source of power.

Finally, the gospel finishes with the message that the Christian life is lived in the presence and in the power of Him who was crucified and rose again. His love made Him venture into a friendship with us: "But as many as received Him, to them gave He power to become the sons of God" (Jn. 1:12a).

B. Love Is a Dedication to an Old Relationship

New relationships can grow into a fellowship and on into comradeship. Soon a new relationship matures and becomes an old relationship. It continues to be not only a redemptive fellowship, but also a healing fellowship. The hymnist was on target when he penned these words: "Blest be the tie that binds our hearts in Christian love."

Luke, in describing the Church at work in Acts, says, "And they continued stedfastly in the apostles' doctrine and fellowship, and in breaking of bread, and in prayers" (Acts 2:42). There were three things that cemented their dedication to Christlike relationships:

1. The truth: The Holy Spirit was carrying out His mission. Jesus had promised that He (the Holy Spirit) would bring to the remembrance of the apostles all the teachings of Jesus and open their minds and hearts to a new truth suited for the new dispensation.

2. The tie: New loves were discovered and established. It was established by doctrines. Precept always

comes before practice. We do not test doctrine by experience, but we do test our experiences by doctrine.

3. The table: The covenant meal would be focal point of their continued communing and communication with Jesus. Love is an adventure into new relationships; it is a dedication to old relationships.

C. Love Is a Sacrifice for a Broken Relationship

This is the practical definition of redemptive love: love that is willing to accept pain for the object of our love. Jesus was the embodiment of this concept.

1. Jesus demonstrated a dedication to old relationships. "He came unto His own, and His own received Him not" (Jn. 1:11).

2. He ventured into new relationships. "But as many as received Him, to them gave He power to become the sons of God, even to them that believe on His name" (Jn. 1:12).

3. He sacrificed for broken relationships. "...If this cup may not pass away from Me, except I drink it, Thy will be done" (Mt. 26:42).

Day Three

Part One

Satan, the Adversary

To begin this third day in our seminars, we ask this question: "How many have reached the point, or hope to reach the point that you can thank God for everything?" Generally most hands will be raised. Then we continue our session by asking a number of questions. These questions are presented here for you to read and consider. Take time to form an answer in your mind. If you would like to, you can write down your responses.

1. If you left this meeting and discovered that someone had put a big dent in your car and had not left a note, would you thank God for your car dent?
2. If the IRS sent you a letter saying that you owed $5,000 in back taxes, would you thank God for the additional taxes?
3. If after your annual physical you were told that you would have to have immediate surgery, would you thank God for surgery?

The purpose for these questions is to get people to admit that they hold God responsible for everything that happens to them. This completely exonerates the devil, and gives him a free hand to create all kinds of problems in our lives.

The word *satan* (pronounced: sa-'tan) is transliterated from the Hebrew. A word that has been transliterated carries forward the sound of the word in the original language, but it does not convey the meaning. In order to convey the meaning, the New Testament writers would need to translate the word. In Hebrew it means "an adversary" and it is used in the Old Testament in a number of passages.

1. It is used of an angel of Jehovah in Numbers 22:22 (the first occurrence of the word in the Old Testament).
2. It is used of men in First Samuel 29:4 and Psalms 71:13; 109:6.
3. It is used of "satan," the devil, in Zechariah 3:1, where the name receives its interpretation, "to be (his) adversary."

In Hebrew the word *satan* simply means "an adversary." It can often be used of men. A man's adversary is his *satan*. In the King James Version, the Philistines were afraid that David would turn out to be their satan (see 1 Sam. 29:4). Solomon declared that God gave him such peace and prosperity that there was no *satan* left to oppose him (see 1 Kings 5:4). David regarded Abishai as his *satan* (see 2 Sam. 19:22). In all these cases *satan* means an adversary or opponent. Another way the word *satan* is used is to designate one who pleads a case against some-one. These are all descriptive uses of the word as it applies to events that happen on earth.

The Jews had the idea that there was an angel in Heaven who had the charge to state a case against a man, a kind of prosecuting angel. The word *satan* was capitalized and became a personal name for this adversary. This is not meant to imply that this adversary, satan, is an evil power from the Jewish perspective. He is simply a part of the judgment apparatus of Heaven. In Job 1:6, satan is numbered among the sons of God: "Now there was a day when the sons of God came to present themselves before the Lord, and Satan came also among them." At this stage satan is the divine prosecutor of man.

But it is not so very far from stating a case against man to making up a case against man, and that is the next step. The Greek language has another word for a supreme evil being, *diabolos* (pronounced: di-ab-o-los), which is translated "devil." It means "slanderer." This has become an alternate name for satan. So satan or the devil is the slanderer par excellence, the adversary of man, the power who is out to frustrate the purposes of God and to ruin mankind. Satan emerges as the enemy who stands for everything that is anti-man and anti-God.

It is from his ruinous power that Jesus teaches us to pray to be delivered. The origin of that power is not discussed and there are no speculations in the New Testament. "If a man wakes up and finds his house on fire, he does not sit down in a chair and write or read a treatise on the origin of fires in private houses. He attempts to try to extinguish the fire and to save his house." So the Bible wastes no time in speculations about the origin of evil. It offers instructions to man so he can fight the battle against evil.

Forms and Sources of Temptation

People are always under attack from temptation, but no enemy can launch an invasion until he finds a bridgehead. Where does temptation find a bridgehead? Where do our temptations come from? To be forewarned is to be forearmed and, if we know from where the attack is likely to come, we will have a better chance of overcoming it.

1. Sometimes the attack of temptation comes from outside us. There are people whose influence is bad. There are people in whose company it would be very difficult even to suggest doing a dishonorable thing, and there are people in whose company it would be easy to do the wrong thing.

Robert Burns tells of his life as a young man. At one point he went to Irvine, Texas, to learn flax-dressing. There he fell in with a certain Robert Brown, a man who had seen much of the world, and who had a fascinating and dominating personality. Burns tells us that he admired him and strove to imitate him. Burns said, "He was the only man I ever saw who was a greater fool than myself when woman was the guiding star—He spoke of a certain fashionable failing with levity, which hitherto I had regarded with horror...Here his friendship did me a mischief."[1]

---

1. *Sermon Illustrations for Windows*, by NAVPRESS, P.O. Box 6000, Colorado Springs, CO 80934. Used by permission.

There are friendships and associations that offer only opportunities to do mischief. In a world filled with temptations, a man should be careful in his choice of friends and of the society in which he moves. He should give the temptations that come from outside as little chance as possible.

2. It is one of the tragic facts of life that temptations can come to us from those who love us. Of all the different kinds of temptation, this is the hardest to fight. It comes from people who love us and who have not the slightest intention of harming us.

A man may know that he ought to take a certain course of action. He may feel drawn to a certain career, but to follow that course of action may involve risk. To accept that career may be to give up all that the world calls success. It may be that in such circumstances those who love him will seek to dissuade him from acting as he knows he ought—and they will do so because of their love for him. They counsel caution, prudence, worldly wisdom; they want to see the one they love do well in a worldly sense; they do not wish to see him throw his chances away—so they seek to stop him from doing what he knows to be right for him.

Jesus said, "And a man's foes shall be they of his own household" (Mt. 10:36). His family came and tried to take Him home because they said that He was mad (see Mk. 3:21). To them, He seemed to be throwing His life and His career away; to them He seemed to be making a fool of Himself. Thus they tried to stop Him. Sometimes the most bitter of all temptations come to us from the voice of love.

3. There is one very odd way in which temptation can come, especially to younger people. For some reason, there is a kind of paradox in many of us that makes us want to appear worse than we are. We do not wish to appear soft and pious, namby-pamby and holy. We would rather be thought of as daredevils, swashbuckling adventurers, men of the world and not innocents.

Augustine has a famous passage in his confessions:

> "Among my equals I was ashamed of being less shameless than others, when I heard them boast of their wickedness...And I took pleasure not only in the pleasure of the deed but in the praise...I made myself worse than I was, that I might not be reproached, and when in anything I had not sinned as the most abandoned ones, I would say that I had done what I had not done, that I might not seen contemptible."

Many a man has started to indulge himself or introduced himself to some habit because he did not wish to appear less experienced than those around him.

The advent of the movies like *The Godfather* with all of its shootings and acts of revenge often has a strange effect on our young men. If someone "crosses your path," then take the "Godfather" approach. Promoting this macho image of manhood are the various street gangs so prevalent today. This activity goes under the name of "Gangster Rap." Their activities cause women to be demoralized and encourage violence as though it is a badge of honor. One of the great defenses against temptation is simply the courage to be good.

4. Temptation comes not only from outside us, it also comes from inside us. If there was nothing in us to which temptation could appeal, then it would be helpless to defeat us. In every one of us there is some weak spot against which temptation launches its attack.

In each of us the point of vulnerability differs. A violent temptation to one man leaves another man quite unmoved; what leaves one man quite unmoved may be an irresistible temptation to another. In every man this weak spot, if left unguarded, can ruin his life. Every man has at least one flaw, some fault of temperament that can ruin his life—some instinct or passion so strong that it may, at any time, snap the leash. We all have some quirk in our makeup that is a pleasure to one and a menace to another. We should identify our areas of weakness and guard them so we can keep them under control.

5. Strangely enough, temptation often comes not from our weakest point, but from our strongest point. One of the most common statements we make is, "That is one thing I would never do." History is full of the stories of castles that were taken just at the point where the defenders thought it so strong that no guard was necessary. Nothing gives temptation its chance like overconfidence. We must always be on guard for an attack of temptation at any time.

The Activities of Satan

Satan's activities are many. He is busy in the life of both believers and non-believers. Listed below are just a few of his activities:

1. He can cause lunacy and mania (see Mt. 4:24).

2. He can cause people to be fierce, unruly, and violent (see Mt. 8:28).
3. He can cause blindness and muteness (see Mt. 9:27-30,33).
4. He can cause discord and divisions (see Mt. 13:24-30,37-42).
5. He can cause grievous vexations (see Mt. 15:22).
6. He can cause self-destruction (see Mt. 17:15).

The Bible is clear that God provides the tools necessary to overcome the onslaught of satan. He gives us the means to combat him both internally and externally.

Externally, in all of his attacks on us, the Word of God is the perfect weapon. Jesus, at the scene of the temptation, demonstrated the successful method of dealing with the devil. In Matthew's Gospel, chapter 4, we see the Master one on one with the devil. Pay particular attention to the words "it is written" in this passage.

But He answered and said, It is written, Man shall not live by bread alone, but by every word that proceedeth out of the mouth of God. ... Jesus said unto him, It is written again, Thou shalt not tempt the Lord thy God. ... Then saith Jesus unto him, Get thee hence, Satan: for it is written, Thou shalt worship the Lord thy God, and Him only shalt thou serve (Matthew 4:4,7,10).

Day Three

Part Two

Being Equipped for the Battle

The Word of God as a Weapon

As an internal weapon, Jesus gave us the power of prayer. It is clear that we are, by God's Word, told how to pray and what to pray for; He gave us principles to follow when we pray.

A. How to Pray

In John's Gospel, chapter 16, Jesus talks about two periods of time: in this day (while He was with them) and in that day (when He would no longer be with them). His instructions were clear on what to do in "that" day, which is now. The Christian prayer is to the Father in Jesus' name.

And in that day ye shall ask Me nothing. Verily, verily, I say unto you, Whatsoever ye shall ask the Father in My name, He will give it you (John 16:23).

B. What to Pray For

When we go to the Lord in prayer, there are three principles that should guide our thought process as we seek fulfillment of our prayer.

1. We are to pray for what we need. "Let us therefore come boldly unto the throne of grace, that we may obtain mercy, and find grace to help in time of need" (Heb. 4:16).

2. We are to pray for what we want. "For the administration of this service not only supplieth the want of the saints, but is abundant also by many thanksgivings unto God" (2 Cor. 9:12).

3. We are to pray for what we desire. "Therefore I say unto you, What things soever ye desire, when ye pray, believe that ye receive them, and ye shall have them" (Mk. 11:24).

Prayer as the Line of Communication

As we offer our prayers to God, there are also certain principles we should keep in mind. I have found five principles that I would like to share with you. They have helped me in my prayer life and I am sure they will be a blessing to you.

1. Adoration: We tell God we regard Him with the utmost respect and love.
2. Confession: We state positively that we approach Him boldly in Jesus' name.
3. Thanksgiving: We recognize that we are the beneficiaries of His grace and mercy each.
4. Supplication: Our prayer for those who are the last, the lost, and the least.
5. Surrender: We submit ourselves to Him to be His agents for good.

Faith Sets the Tone for Success

Although these are the basic principles, I also feel that I must share with you some of my other discoveries concerning prayer. I will call these additional principles, "Ten Rules for 100% Answered Prayer" to distinguish them from the five basic principles just noted.

1. Have complete faith in the promises of God. Our faith must be strong enough to hold. If God made the promise, He will keep His promise. God's covenant, His oath, is immutable (it cannot be changed). Therefore, we can talk about His future promises as if they were already accomplished—in the past tense. Occasionally I will receive the comment, "Well, even though He promises us whatsoever, sometimes the Lord says no." I have not found a Scripture where God said, "No!" in relationship to a promise that He has made. I do recall His Word in Second Corinthians 1:20: "For all the promises of God in Him are yea, and in Him Amen, unto the glory of God by us."

Wherein God, willing more abundantly to shew unto the heirs of promise the immutability of His counsel, confirmed it by an oath: that by two immutable things, in which it was impossible for God to lie, we might have a strong consolation, who have fled for refuge to lay hold upon the hope set before us: which hope we have as an anchor of the soul, both sure and stedfast, and which entereth into that within the veil (Hebrews 6:17-19).

The writer to the Hebrews uses a most illuminating word about Jesus. He says that He entered the presence of God as our forerunner. The word is *prodromos*. Basically, it has two stages of meaning:

(a) It means one who rushes on, a pioneer.

(b) It means a scout who goes ahead to see that it is safe for the body of the troops to follow. Jesus went into the presence of God to make it safe for all men to follow.

Let me put it very simply in another way. Before Jesus came, God was a distant stranger whom only a few dared to approach—and that at peril of their lives. But because of who Jesus was and what He did, God became the friend of every man. Once men thought of God as barring the door. Now they see the door to His presence as wide open to all.

2. Say in no uncertain terms what you want from God. I often tell my audiences that, when I petition God, I tell Him the manufacturer's name, model number, make, and color.

> *For verily I say unto you, That whosoever shall say unto this mountain, Be thou removed, and be thou cast into the sea; and shall not doubt in his heart, but shall believe that those things which he saith shall come to pass; he shall have whatsoever he saith* (Mark 11:23).

This passage gives us three rules for prayer.

(a) It must be the prayer of faith. The phrase about removing mountains was a common Jewish phrase. It was especially used of wise teachers. A good teacher who could remove the difficulties that the minds of his scholars encountered was called a mountain-remover. One who heard a famous rabbi teach said that he saw Resh Lachish as if he were plucking up mountains. So the phrase means that if we have faith, prayer is a power that can solve any problem and make us able to deal with any difficulty. That sounds very simple, but it involves two things.

First, we should be willing to take our problems and our difficulties to God. That in itself is a very real test. Sometimes our problems are not valid and involve requests to satisfy misplaced desires, to do something we should not be doing, or to justify a wrong action. One of the greatest tests of any problem is simply to say, "Can I take it to God and can I ask for His help?"

Second, we should be ready to accept God's guidance when He gives it. It is a common thing for a person to ask for advice when all he really wants is approval for some action that he is about to take or has already taken. It is useless to go to God and to ask for His guidance unless we are willing to be obedient to His answer. If we take our problems to God and are humble enough and brave enough to accept His guidance, we will receive the power to conquer the difficulties of thought and of action.

(b) It must be the prayer of expectation. It is a universal fact that anything tried in the spirit of confident expectation has more than double the chance of success. The patient who goes to a doctor and has no confidence in the prescribed remedies has far less chance of recovery than the patient who is confident that the doctor will succeed. When we pray, it must never be a mere formality. It must never be a ritual without hope. Unfortunately,

for many people prayer is either a pious ritual or a shot
in the dark. Our prayers should burn with expectation.
Maybe our trouble is that what we want from God is *our*
answer, and we do not recognize *His* answer when it
comes.

(c) It must be a prayer of charity. The prayer of a bitter man cannot penetrate the wall of his own bitterness.
Why? The first principle of God is love, for He is love. If
the ruling principle of a man's heart is bitterness, he has
erected a barrier between himself and God. If the prayer
of such a man is to be answered, he must first ask God to
cleanse his heart of his bitter spirit and replace it with a
spirit of love. Then he can speak to God and God can
speak to him.

3. Have faith without qualifying God's promises. Too
often I hear in seminars and institutes such expressions
as "God only promised what we need." Mark's Gospel
says, "what things soever ye desire." God does not limit
Himself. Throughout the Bible, He uses such terms as
"whatsoever" or "anything" to demonstrate how much
He wants to fill our every need.

"Jesus said unto him, If thou canst believe, all things
are possible to him that believeth" (Mk. 9:23). In this
verse Jesus was addressing the father whose son lay sick
and near death. Often the words of Jesus are misunder-
stood. In my seminars, I take time to point out the elements of this statement so people will stop using their
lack of understanding as an excuse for their unbelief.

To the father of the boy Jesus stated the conditions of
a miracle. "To him who believes," said Jesus, "all things

are possible." It was as if Jesus said, "The cure of your boy depends not on Me, but on you." To approach anything in the spirit of hopelessness is to make it hopeless; to approach anything in the spirit of faith is to make it a possibility. Cavour once said that what a statesman needed above all was "a sense of the possible." Most of us are cursed with a sense of the impossible, and that is precisely why miracles do not happen.

The whole attitude of the father of the boy is most illuminating. Originally, he had come seeking Jesus himself. His faith was badly shaken, so badly shaken that when he came to Jesus all he could say at first was, "Help me, if you can." Then, as he confronted Jesus face to face, suddenly his faith blazed up again. "I believe," he cried. It was if he were saying, "If there is still some discouragement in me, still some doubts, take them away and fill me with an unquestioning faith."

Sometimes people get less than they hoped for from some church or from some servant of the church. When that happens they ought to press beyond the church to the Master of the church, beyond the servant of Christ to Christ Himself. Our church may at times disappoint us, and God's servants on earth may disappoint us. But when we battle our way face to face with Jesus Christ, He never disappoints us.

4. Refuse satan the opportunity to place doubt in your heart about the answer to your prayer. Satan is a master of deception and his favorite ploy is to convince the believer that he does not deserve the thing for which he is asking. There is nothing in God's promises that limits His love and goodness.

And Jesus said unto them, Because of your unbelief: for verily I say unto you, If ye have faith as a grain of mustard seed, ye shall say unto this mountain, Remove hence to yonder place; and it shall remove; and nothing shall be impossible unto you (Matthew 17:20).

5. In your private prayer life, pray only specific prayers. General prayers are a necessary part of public worship, but one-on-one prayer with God requires specifics. After all, this is a child talking to his parent.

Ask, and it shall be given you; seek, and ye shall find; knock, and it shall be opened unto you: for every one that asketh receiveth; and he that seeketh findeth; and to him that knocketh it shall be opened (Matthew 7:7-8).

The word *ask* in the Greek (*aitero*) means "to crave, to desire with passion." It is to focus all of your energy momentarily and then direct this energy on your prayer petition.

There is a vital lesson here. God will always answer our prayers, but He will answer them in His way. His way will be the way of perfect wisdom and of perfect love. If He answered all our prayers instantly, it would be the worst thing possible for us. Too often in our ignorance we ask for gifts that would lead to our ruin. The words of Jesus in the verse just quoted (Mt. 7:7-8) tell us that God will not only answer, but also answer in wisdom and in love.

To understand these words more fully, I need to make you aware of the two ways the Greek language can express a command. In Greek, commands are in the imperative. There are two kinds of imperatives that are used. The first is the aorist imperative, which is a single definite command like, "Shut the door behind you." This is spoken one time for a single event.

Then there is the present imperative; it issues a command that requires continuing action, such as, "Always shut the door behind you." In recording the words of Jesus, the writers and translators used the present imperative. They understood the words of Jesus to mean, "Go on asking; go on seeking; go on knocking." He is telling us to persist in prayer, to never be discouraged in prayer. Clearly the test of our sincerity lies within our resolve. Do we really want a thing? The best test of a valid desire is our ability to bring our request into God's presence and to continue to do so with persistence.

6. Believe that whatever you are asking for has already been granted. God's pantry is fully stocked. Only God can afford to say "whatsoever."

Blessed be the God and Father of our Lord Jesus Christ, who hath blessed us with all spiritual blessings in heavenly places in Christ (Ephesians 1:3).

Christians are the chosen people of God. In this verse Paul sets forth three arguments:

(a) He considers the choice to be God's. Paul did not choose to do God's work. He knew that God chose him. Jesus said to His disciples, "Ye have not chosen Me, but I have chosen you..." (Jn. 15:16). It is not so wonderful for man to choose God—the wonder is that God chose man.

(b) Paul recognizes the bounty of God's choice. God chose us to bless us with heavenly blessings. There are certain things a man can discover for himself, but there are others that are beyond his grasp. A man can acquire a certain skill, achieve a certain position, and amass a certain amount of this world's goods, but he can never attain to goodness or to peace of mind without God's help. God chose us to give us those things that He alone can give.

(c) Paul sees the purpose of God's choice. God chose us to be holy and blameless. God has made us blameless by reckoning Jesus' blameless life to us. He has made us holy, set apart to be vessels of His continuing work with His creation.

7. Be authoritative and command to come to pass the thing you are petitioning.

> *And Jesus said unto them, Because of your unbelief: for verily I say unto you, If ye have faith as a grain of mustard seed, ye shall say unto this mountain, Remove hence to yonder place; and it shall remove; and nothing shall be impossible unto you* (Matthew 17:20).

This verse expresses the central need of faith, without which nothing can happen. When Jesus spoke about removing mountains, He was using a phrase the Jews knew well. A great teacher who could expound and interpret Scripture and who could explain and resolve difficulties, was regularly known as an uprooter or a pulverizer of mountains. Phrases like "to tear up, to uproot, to pulverize" were phrases regularly used to describe one who could resolve difficulties.

Jesus never meant these phrases to be understood literally. What He meant was this: "If you have enough faith, all difficulties can be solved and even the hardest task can be accomplished." Faith in God is the instrument that enables men to remove the hills of difficulty that block their path.

8. Believe that what you want is God's will. It stands to reason that one cannot argue for what is contrary to God's will.

> *According as His divine power hath given unto us all things that pertain unto life and godliness, through the knowledge of Him that hath called us to glory and virtue: whereby are given unto us exceeding great and precious promises: that by these ye might be partakers of the divine nature, having escaped the corruption that is in the world through lust* (2 Peter 1:3).

9. Have a clean life with God and man. Remember that God sees all believers as His family. His children demonstrate their love for Him by loving one another.

> *And when ye stand praying, forgive, if ye have aught against any: that your Father also which is in heaven may forgive you your trespasses. But if ye do not forgive, neither will your Father which is in heaven forgive your trespasses* (Mark 11:25).

> *But whoso hath this world's good, and seeth his brother have need, and shutteth up his bowels of compassion from him, how dwelleth the love of God in him? My little children, let us not love in word, neither in tongue; but in deed and in truth* (1 John 3:17-18).

10. Give God His tithe as an act of appreciation and love. To give unselfishly demonstrates your desire to participate in building His Kingdom.

Day Three

Part Three

Kingdom Responsibilities and Rewards

Three Conditions for Rewards

Some people are critical that an overemphasis on God's promises means people are serving God only for the rewards offered. This argument is generally backed up by such Scriptures as this:

> *Take heed that ye do not your alms before men, to be seen of them: otherwise ye have no reward of your Father which is in heaven. Therefore when thou doest thine alms, do not sound a trumpet before thee, as the hypocrites do in the synagogues and in the streets, that they may have glory of men. Verily I say unto you, They have their reward. But when thou doest alms, let not thy left hand know what thy right hand doeth: that thine alms may be in secret: and thy Father which seeth in secret Himself shall reward thee openly* (Matthew 6:1-4).

This principle is so important that we should stop and take a closer look at Matthew 6. Some believe that any motivation toward reward has no place in Christian life. These people believe we must be good for the sake of being good, that virtue is its own reward, and that the whole concept of reward be abolished. There was an old saint who used to say that he would wish to quench all the fires of hell with water and to burn up all the joys of Heaven with fire so men would seek goodness for no other reason than goodness' sake. He wanted the idea of reward and punishment totally eliminated from life.

On the surface this point of view may seem fine and noble, but it is contrary to the point of view which Jesus held. Three times in this passage alone, Jesus speaks of reward. The right kind of almsgiving, the right kind of prayer, and the right kind of fasting will all have their reward. In another passage, Jesus says that those who bear persecution and those who suffer insult without bitterness, will receive great rewards in Heaven (see Mt. 5:11-12). He also said that whoever gives to one of these little ones a cup of cold water in the name of a disciple will not lose his reward (see Mt. 10:42). In the parable of the talents, faithful service will receive its reward (see Mt. 25:14-30). In the parable of the last judgment, reward and punishment will be administered in accordance with our reaction to the needs of our fellow men (see Mt. 25:31-46).

Reward and Punishment in the Christian Life

It is clear that Jesus did not hesitate to speak in terms of rewards and punishments. We should be careful not to be more spiritual than Jesus in our complaints about this matter of reward. Perhaps these facts are worth mentioning:

1. It is an obvious rule of life that any action that achieves nothing is futile and meaningless. A good deed that achieves no result would be a meaningless deed. As it has been said, "Unless a thing is good for something, it is good for nothing." Unless the Christian life has an aim and a goal, it is largely without meaning. He who believes in the Christian way and the Christian promise cannot believe that goodness can have no result beyond itself.

2. To banish all rewards and punishments from the idea of religion says, in effect, that injustice has the last word. It cannot reasonably be held that the end of the good man and the end of the bad man are one and the same. That would mean God does not care whether men are good or not. It would mean, to put it crudely and bluntly, there is no point in being good and no compelling reason why a man should live one kind of life instead of another. To eliminate all rewards and punishments is really to say that in God there is neither justice nor love. Rewards and punishments are necessary in order to make sense of life. There are certain things about this, however, which we must be clear.

(a) When Jesus spoke of reward, He was not thinking in terms of material reward. It is quite true that in the Old Testament the idea of goodness and prosperity are closely connected. If a man prospered, if his fields were fertile and his harvest great, if his children were many and his fortune large, it was taken as a proof that he was a good man.

That is precisely the problem at the end of the Book of Job. Job suffered misfortune and his friends come to him to argue that misfortune must be the result of his own sin. Job vehemently denies that charge. "Remember, I pray thee," said Eliphaz, "who ever perished, being innocent?" (Job 4:7a) "If thou wert pure and upright," said Bildad, "surely now He would awake for thee, and make the habitation of thy righteousness prosperous" (Job 8:6). "For Thou hast said, My doctrine is pure, and I am clean in Thine eyes,' " said Zophar. "But oh that God would speak, and open His lips against thee" (Job 11:4-5). The Book of Job was written to contradict the idea that goodness and material prosperity go hand in hand.

> *I have been young, and now am old; yet have I not seen the righteous forsaken, nor his seed begging bread* (Psalm 37:25).

> *A thousand shall fall at thy side, and ten thousand at thy right hand; but it shall not come nigh thee. Only with thine eyes shalt thou behold and see the reward of the wicked. Because thou hast made the LORD, which is my refuge, even the most High, thy habitation; there shall no evil befall thee, neither shall any plague come nigh thy dwelling* (Psalm 91:7-10).

These are things that Jesus could never have said. It was certainly not material prosperity that Jesus promised His disciples. He in fact promised them trial and tribulation, suffering, persecution, and death. Quite certainly Jesus did not think in terms of material rewards.

(b) The second thing it is necessary to remember is that the highest reward never comes to the one who is seeking it. If a man is always seeking reward, always adding up his deeds, then he will surely miss the reward he is seeking. He will miss it because he is looking at God and looking at life in the wrong way. A man who is always calculating his reward is thinking of God in terms of a judge or an accountant. Above all, he is thinking of life in terms of law. He is thinking of doing only so much and earning only so much. He is thinking of life in terms of a credit and debit balance sheet. He is thinking of presenting his account to God, saying, "I have done so much. Now I claim my reward."

The basic mistake in this point of view is that life is seen in terms of law instead of love. If we love a person deeply, passionately, humbly, and selflessly, we will be sure that when we give that person all we have to give, we will still not have given enough. If we give that person the sun, the moon, and the stars, we will still be in debt. He who is in love is always in debt. The last thing that enters his mind is earning a reward. If a man has a legal view of life, he thinks constantly in terms of his winnings. If a man has a loving view of life, the idea of reward will never enter his mind.

The great paradox of Christian reward is this: The person who looks for reward and who calculates what is due him, does not receive it. On the other hand, the person whose only motive is love and who never thinks that he has deserved any reward, does receive it. Strangely, a reward is at one and the same time the by-product and the ultimate end of the Christian life.

3. What are the rewards of the Christian life?

We begin by noting one basic, universal truth. We have already seen that Jesus Christ does not think in

terms of material reward at all. The rewards of the Christian
life are rewards for those concerned with spiritual results.
To the materially-minded person they would not be rewards at all. Christian rewards apply only to a Christian.

(a) The first reward of a Christian is satisfaction. Doing the right thing, obeying Jesus Christ, following the
Christian ethic, regardless of recognition or cost, always
brings satisfaction. It may well be that, if a man does the
right thing and obeys Jesus Christ, he may lose his fortune
and his position. He may be unpopular, lonely, and in
disrepute, but he will still possess that inner satisfaction.

(b) The second reward of the Christian life is the work
that is yet to be done. One of the paradoxes of Christian
reward is that a task well done does not bring rest, comfort, and ease. Instead, it brings greater demands and requires more strenuous effort. In the parable of the
talents, the reward of the faithful servants was added responsibility (see Mt. 25:14-30). When a teacher gets a
brilliant and able scholar, he does not exempt that stu-
dent from work; he gives that person harder work than
he gives to his less capable students. The brilliant young
musician is given more difficult music to master. The lad
who has played well on the second string is not put back
to third string. He is advanced to the first string where
his skill can be tested.

The Jews have a curious saying. They say a wise
teacher will treat the pupil "like a young heifer whose
burden is increased daily." The Christian reward is the
reverse of the world's reward. The world's reward would
be an easier time; the reward of the Christian is that God

lays more upon a man to do for his fellow men. The harder the work we are given to do, the greater the reward.

(c) The final Christian reward is often called the vision of God. The worldly man who has never given a thought to God, when confronted by God, will be filled with terror. If a man goes his own way, he drifts farther and farther from God. The gulf between him and God becomes ever wider, until in the end God becomes a stranger to avoid at all costs. But if a man seeks to walk with God all his life, if he has tried to obey his Lord, if goodness has been his quest through all his days, then all his life he has been growing closer and closer to God and in the end he passes into God's presence. He will enjoy God's presence without fear and with radiant joy. This final reward is the greatest reward of all.

Day Four

Part One

Identifying and Dealing
With Problems in the Church

As we begin our fourth day in the seminar sessions, we begin to focus on some of the problems that arise within a growing church community. If you read the Book of Acts carefully, you will notice several times where dissension or various problems arose that required attention. I mentioned one such problem earlier when we discussed the need for the office of deacon in the early Church.

As an entry into the discussion of problems with the church today, I would like to begin with a story about a boy named Jo. I think we can gain some insight into the questions that face the Church if we have an example to set the stage for our discussion.

A Boy Named Jo

There is a 13-year-old boy back in the "bush" in Africa. He has never seen a Bible, never heard a sermon, never been told the story of Jesus and the salvation He offers. He has never seen a church and he has never been confronted with anything having to do with Christianity.

First let me ask this question: Is Jo saved or lost? Some will contend that Jo is saved; some will say he is lost; and some will simply hedge or compromise on the answer.

Now let me add another element and ask a second question. Suppose we send a missionary to the bush country and our missionary tells Jo the story of Jesus. At the end of the story our missionary asks Jo to accept Jesus as his personal Savior, but Jo refuses. Is Joe lost or saved?

If we conclude that Jo is lost, can we also conclude our missionary, who went to witness to Jo, caused him to be lost?

You may say that this is either a difficult exercise or you may think the exercise frivolous. Yet if we look back to the community (*koinonia*) in the Book of Acts, we find that, in the early stages, it is organized with officers, deacons, and members who know the work of Jesus must be continued. For a while all is well in the community. Then, beginning with Acts 6, we find a group who is not happy with the way things are being done.

> *And in those days, when the number of the disciples was multiplied, there arose a murmuring of the Grecians against the Hebrews, because their widows were neglected in the daily ministration. Then the twelve called the multitude of the disciples unto them, and said, It is not reason that we should leave the word of God, and*

serve tables. Wherefore, brethren, look ye out among you seven men of honest report, full of the Holy Ghost and wisdom, whom we may appoint over this business. But we will give ourselves continually to prayer, and to the ministry of the word (Acts 6:1-4).

Relationship Problems in the Koinonia

The Church had a problem with dissension. As the Church grew, dissension and grumbling increased. We assume that church growth is the goal of any congregation, yet a closer examination of the attitude of the original organizers of our local churches seems contrary to that assumption. We can learn and be encouraged from this story of problems in the fledgling church founded by the disciples of Jesus. We can see that in every church there is a mixture of good and bad. There are always members in a church (good people) who would rather maintain the status quo. Church growth can be threatening to even the most faithful of followers. Wherever there is a dying church, it is because the controlling faction in the church wants things to "stay as they are."

When a church becomes stagnant or starts the process of losing membership, it is not because of the forces outside the church. All it takes to kill a church is a strong group of Christians doing nothing. The problem described in Acts 6 arose because the pastors were accused of showing favoritism.

In the synagogue of the first century it was a routine custom to send two collectors to the market and to private homes every Friday morning. Their job was to collect for the needy. They would routinely receive a combination of money and goods. Later in the day this was distributed. Some had a temporary need and they received enough to see them through their period of lack. Others were permanent cases, those who were unable to support themselves, and they received enough for 14 meals or a week's provisions. The fund from which this distribution was made was called the *Kuppah* or Basket.

In addition to the weekly collection, often a daily collection was necessary. This was done from house-to-house for those who had an emergency or a pressing need. This was called the *Tamhui*, or Tray. The conflict arose because the distribution was not reaching a segment of the community. This failure in administration led to a second problem.

The Church had a problem with neglect. The newly formed Christian community (the *Koinonia*) continued the Jewish custom of collection and distribution. But there was a division or split in the membership. There were two different sects of Jews. The Jerusalem and the Palestinian Jews spoke Hebrew and Aramaic and were proud that no foreign influence had tainted their lives. There were also Hellenistic Jews, who had come for Pentecost from outside of Palestine (Israel). Many of these had been away from Palestine for generations and, having forgotten their Hebrew, they spoke only Greek.

This language problem caused the local Jews to look down upon the other Greek-speaking Jews. This contempt affected the daily distribution of alms and there was a complaint that the widows of the Greek-speaking Jews were being neglected, possibly on purpose.

This story shows that even in the early Church there were imperfect Christians. True to its nature, the Bible tells us about both the good and the bad in people and in the Church. Once a court painter painted a portrait of Oliver Cromwell. Cromwell was disfigured by warts upon his face. The painter, thinking to please the great man, omitted the disfiguring warts. When Cromwell saw the picture, he said, "Take it away, and paint me warts and all." It is one of the great virtues of the Bible that it shows us its heroes, warts and all.

The Church had a problem with class distinction. There was neglect and that neglect seems to have been based on bigotry. We have no indication of how much time had elapsed since the inception of the Christian community, but we can see that the number of disciples was increasing. The Church continued to grow (see Acts 5:14), which gave rise to concerns, both from within (see Acts 6:1-7) and from without (see Acts 6:8–7:60). At this stage of its development, the Church membership was predominately Jews. However, there were two distinct groups of Jews within the fellowship; one group felt neglected.

Identifying the Conflicting Groups

1. Hebraic Jews: Those who spoke the Hebrew or Aramaic and sought to preserve Jewish culture and customs. Help was needed by those widows who had no one to care for them and so they became the Church's responsibility (see Acts 4:35; 11:28-29).

2. Hellenistic Jews: There were also Jews from other countries and most of them had been away from Palestine for generations. They had been born in lands other

than Palestine and their main language was Greek. They were not nearly so strict about Jewish custom, since their attitudes and outlook were colored by the Greek rather than Jewish culture.

Leadership Problems in the Koinonia

There was the problem of doctrines.

And certain men which came down from Judaea taught the brethren, and said, Except ye be circumcised after the manner of Moses, ye cannot be saved. When therefore Paul and Barnabas had no small dissension and disputation with them, they determined that Paul and Barnabas, and certain other of them, should go up to Jerusalem unto the apostles and elders about this question (Acts 15:1-2).

In Antioch, almost by accident, the gospel was being preached to Jew and Gentile alike. The two were living together as brethren. This disturbed a number of the Jews, who were determined to enforce their own customs on the new converts. Even though they maintained the position of the Jews as the chosen people of God, they were quite willing for the Gentiles to join the community. But they had a condition: First they must accept the Jewish rite of circumcision as evidence of their conversion. If this attitude had prevailed, Christianity would have become nothing other than a sect of Judaism. Some of these narrow-minded Jews came down to Antioch and tried to persuade the converts that they would lose everything unless they first accepted Judaism. Paul and Barnabas argued strongly against this, but they were not able to settle the matter.

There was only one way out. An appeal had to be made to the council of apostles and elders in Jerusalem. These men were recognized as the governing authority and whatever they required would be accepted as the final decision on this issue. Paul and Barnabas returned to Jerusalem and the matter was discussed among the leadership.

Paul and Barnabas gave their report and were prepared to let the facts speak for themselves. But certain believers who were of the Pharisees insisted that all converts must be circumcised and keep the law.

The principle at stake was quite simple. Was the gift of God for the select few or for all the world? If it is meant for the whole world, how is the gift given to those who are not a part of the Jewish community? Is the gift a privilege or a responsibility? The problem may not appear in precisely the same way today, but divisions do exist between nations, races, ethnic groups, and special classes of people. We fully realize the true meaning of Christianity only when all of the walls of partition are broken down.

There was the problem of prejudice. On the surface, the significance of this problem seemed localized and temporary. What seemed to be a problem in the early Church seems to apply only to the past without much relevance for us today. Still, we must not dismiss the issue out of hand. The problems reported in the Book of Acts are of interest because the domestic affairs and problems of the early Church guide us in understanding these same issues in our Church today.

The problem of prejudice centers on the rights and place of women in the early Church. Paul's answer was blunt. The veil is always a sign of subjection. It is worn by an inferior in the presence of a superior. Since woman is inferior to man, who is head of the household, it is therefore wrong for a man to appear at public worship veiled and equally wrong for a woman to appear unveiled. That was Paul's answer. It is not likely, in the twentieth century, that we would accept this view of the inferiority and subordination of women. But we must read this chapter in the light of the first century, not the twentieth century, and as we read it we must remember three things:

1. We must remember the place of the veil in the East. To this day Eastern women wear the *yashmak,* which is a long veil leaving the forehead and the eyes uncovered, but reaching down almost to the feet. In Paul's time the Eastern veil was even more concealing. It came right over the head with only an opening for the eyes. A respectable Eastern woman would never appear in public without it.

Writing in *Hastings' Dictionary of the Bible,* T.W. Davies says, "No respectable woman in an eastern village or city goes out without it, and, if she does, she is in danger of being misjudged. Indeed English and American missionaries in Egypt state that their own wives and daughters when going about find it often best to wear the veil." The veil was two things:

(a) It was a sign of inferiority. It clearly distinguished the place for women.

(b) It was also a great protection. First Corinthians 11:10 is very difficult to translate. We should translate it this way: "For this reason a woman ought to retain upon her head the sign that she is under someone else's authority." The Greek literally means that a woman ought to retain "her authority upon her head."

Sir William Ramsay explains it this way:

> "In Oriental lands the veil is the power and honor and dignity of the woman. With the veil on her head she can go anywhere in security and profound respect. She is not seen and it is a mark of thoroughly bad manners to observe a veiled woman in the street. She is alone. The rest of the people around are non-existent to her, as she is to them. She is supreme in the crowd...But without the veil the woman is a thing of nought, whom anyone may insult...A woman's authority and dignity vanish along with the all-covering veil that she discards."

In the East, then, the veil is all-important. It does not only mark the inferior status of a woman, but it also is the inviolable protection of her modesty and chastity.

2. We must remember the status of women from a Jewish perspective. Under Jewish law women were vastly inferior to men. Woman was created out of Adam's rib (see Gen. 2:22-23) and she had been created to be the help meet of man (see Gen. 2:18). There was a rabbinic piece of fanciful exegesis which said:

"God did not form woman out of the
head lest she should become proud;
nor out of the eye lest she should lust;
nor out of the ear lest she should be
curious; nor out of the mouth lest she
should be talkative; nor out of the
heart lest she should be jealous; nor
out of the hand lest she should be cov-
etous; nor out of the foot lest she
should be a wondering busybody; but
out of a rib which was always covered;
therefore modesty should be her primary quality."[1]

It is an unfortunate truth that in Jewish law a woman
was chattel and, as such, she was the property of her husband. He had complete rights of disposal. In the synagogue, for instance, women had no share whatever in
the worship. They were completely segregated from the
men, separated by a partition or in a separate room or
gallery. In Jewish law and custom it was unthinkable for
women to claim any kind of equality with men. In First
Corinthians 11:10 there is a curious phrase that women
should be veiled "because of the angels." It is not certain
what this means, but probably it goes back to the strange
story in Genesis 6:1-2 which tells how the angels fell prey
to the charms of mortal women and sinned. The idea
may have developed that the unveiled woman is a temptation even to the angels. An old rabbinic tradition which
said that it was the beauty of women's long hair that
tempted the angels, seems to support this opinion.

---

1.   *The Bible Encyclopedia* (J. Mitchell Howard Co., 1901).

3. It must always be remembered that this situation arose in Corinth, one of the most licentious cities in the world. In such a situation Paul must have thought it better to err on the side modesty rather than to do anything that might give the heathen a chance to criticize the Christians. It is inappropriate to apply this passage universally. Still, even though its significance is primarily local and dated, it offers three great permanent truths:

(a) The reasoning behind Paul's position and of the early Church was this: It is always better to err on the side of being too strict than on the side of being too lax. It is far better to abandon rights that may be stumbling blocks. It may be fashionable to decry conventions, but a man should always think twice before he defies it and shocks others. True, one must never be the slave of tradition, but traditions do not usually come into being without reason.

(b) Even after he has stressed the subordination of woman, Paul also stresses more directly the essential partnership of man and woman. Neither can live without the other. If subordination is necessary, it is in order that the partnership may be more fruitful and more lovely for both.

(c) Paul finishes the passage with a rebuke to the man who argues for the sake of argument. Whatever differences may arise between men, there is no place in the Church for the deliberately contentious man or woman. There is a time to stand on principle, but there is no justification for those who persist in arguing selfishly. Where there is unity and peace, there is also room for diversity.

The controversy over the role of women in the service and administration of church work, as well as the work of the Church, is at issue in many established churches today. The most obvious controversy, from a denominational standpoint, is women functioning as priests or clergy. The issue is far from settled. In that there are several books addressing the problems women face in being accepted as clergy in the Church, I will not attempt to address the issue in this book.

Day Four

Part Two

Identifying Sin and Setting Limits

Problems With Sin in the *Koinonia*

There was the problem of sin in the Church. Paul's first letter to the church at Corinth addresses sin in the church. It appears Paul had written a letter to the Corinthians in which he had urged them to avoid associating with evil men. He applied this request to members of the church and as discipline he ordered that the evil men be ejected from the community until they repented. Some took this to be a permanent excommunication. In a place like Corinth it would have been impossible to carry on a normal life if every wrongful act was punished by excommunication. Paul never intended what the Corinthian Christians applied. "God," as the old saint said to John Wesley, "knows nothing of solitary religion," and Paul would have agreed with him.

Paul identified three types or classes of sin. We can assume these to be the most important from Paul's perspective.

1. There are the fornicators, those guilty of lax morality. Christianity alone cannot guarantee purity. The root cause of sexual immorality is a wrong view of humanity. In the end it views men as beasts. It declares that the passions and instincts they share with the beasts must be shamelessly gratified. Futhermore, it regards the other person as a mere instrument through which that gratification may be obtained. Christianity declares man to be a child of God and, as His child, a creature who lives in the world but who always looks beyond life in this world and toward eternal life with the Father. God's children will not live their lives to gratify purely physical needs and desires. They realize they have a physical body, but they are also a spirit and they are led by God's Spirit. If men regarded themselves and others as the sons and daughters of God, moral laxity would automatically be banished from life.

Fornication is a sin against self. By giving into fornication, man reduces himself to the level of an animal. He has sinned against the light that is in him by allowing his lower nature (flesh) to defeat his higher nature (spirit).

2. There are those who are greedy for this world's goods. Once again only Christianity can banish the spirit of greed. If we judge things by purely material standards, there is no reason we should not dedicate our lives to the task of getting all the material goods we can. But Christianity builds up the spirit to find satisfaction in becoming whole rather than acquiring everything. It makes love the highest value in life and service the greatest honor. When the love of God is in a man's heart, he will find his joy not in getting, but in giving.

Greed is a sin against our neighbors and our fellow man. It regards human beings as persons to be exploited rather than as brothers to be helped. It forgets that the only proof of our love of God is our loving our neighbors as ourselves.

Paul ends that discussion with a definite command: "Put away the wicked man from amongst you" (see 1 Cor. 5:13). He is quoting from Deuteronomy 17:7 and 24:7. There are times when a cancer must be cut out. There are times when drastic measures must be taken to avoid infection. It is not the desire to hurt or the wish to show his power that moves Paul. It is the pastor's desire to protect his infant church from the ever-threatening infection of the world.

3. There are the idolaters. Ancient idolatry has its parallel in modern superstition. For ages man has been fascinated with amulets, charms, and occult devices. They have been engrossed in astrology, horoscopes, and astral projections. It is a basic rule of life that a man must worship something. Unless he worships the true God, he will worship the gods of luck. Whenever religion grows weak, superstition grows strong.

Idolatry is a sin against God. It exalts superstition and puts it in God's place. One of Paul's principles is to refrain from judging those outside the Church. "Those outside" is a Jewish phrase used to describe people outside the "chosen people." We must leave their judgment to God, who alone knows the hearts of men. But the man within the Church has special privileges and therefore special responsibilities. He has taken an oath to Christ and can therefore be called into question for how well he keeps his pledge.

Setting Goals and Establishing Priorities

There was the problem of priorities. Up until then the disciples had been of one accord, but now they have increased in number and are starting to murmur. The Word of God was enough to take up all the thoughts, cares, and time of the apostles. The decision had to be made by the apostles as to what it was they were supposed to be doing, and what things were to be given the highest priority.

1. Should they spend their time serving the needs of the local congregation?
2. Should their time be spent on evangelism and missions as they had been charged in Acts 1:8?

This then takes us to the theme of these seminar lectures, "What are we supposed to be doing as a church?" It is apparent that most of the apostles' time was spent in solving local problems—problems that I have termed "church work." Church work required most of their energy and there was little or no time to do the "work of the Church." There is a need for both.

Day Four

Part Three

The Mission of the Church

We Are to Do Church Work

The Church was to create a community in which to
live as new creatures in a new life. Their training and
growth would certainly be enhanced by living in a close
fellowship where the members of the community observed the same moral and social practices. It was a
"community of the redeemed." To maintain the community, it had to be managed as though it was one large
household. Tasks had to be assigned; responsibilities had
to be assumed. They shared in the work and mainte-
nance of the "community." Each bore his own share of
the work, and "they had all things common."

These activities were expanded as time passed and, as
their numbers grew, their needs grew. We can find a parallel for this in the local church today. We have boards,
leadership groups, and department heads. The Sunday
school, choir, ushers, guilds, and social groups are all

involved in doing the church work. Maintaining the financial, social, moral, and doctrinal functions of the *Koinonia* is also church work. Still, these are essential services that make the church a place with something for everyone. That is what community is all about—serving the needs of all and all serving to fill the needs.

We Are to Do the Work of the Church

> *But ye shall receive power, after that the Holy Ghost is come upon you: and ye shall be witnesses unto Me both in Jerusalem, and in all Judaea, and in Samaria, and unto the uttermost part of the earth* (Acts 1:8).

If the Church is to do church work *only*, then the Church becomes a New Testament type of the Jewish synagogue. The Church began as a purely Jewish institution. The apostles seemed satisfied to keep the Church local and limited. This is not what Jesus had in mind when He told them to go into the world with the good news. So God used a growing persecution of the Church to get the message out to the world.

The beginning of the persecution is best seen in the horrible death of Stephen, which took place under the watchful eye of the high priest in Jerusalem. With such approval from the high priest and the Sanhedrin (Jewish legal council), the persecutions increased, causing all but the apostles to leave Jerusalem and go out into Judea and Samaria. From this point forward, two important changes take place in the position and direction of the Church.

The First Missionaries

Philip and the Samaritans. The gospel had been preached mostly in Jerusalem to Jews. The first big change was the preaching of the gospel to the people of Samaria (see Acts 8). The Samaritans were hated by the Jews because they were half-Jew and half-Gentile. This mixture was due to the loss of the Northern Kingdom to the Assyrians in 8 B.C. The hatred had continued for more than 800 years and contact was discouraged by the religious leaders.

When Philip left Jerusalem, he ended up in Samaria. There he preached the gospel with power. Many were baptized, both men and women, and there were great signs and wonders of healings and deliverance. Even though the Samaritans were considered second-class Jews at best, Peter and John were sent to Samaria when word reached Jerusalem. When they arrived, they prayed for those who had been baptized and they were all filled with the Holy Spirit. Philip, at the urging of the Holy Spirit, then headed south and on the way he encountered an Ethiopian eunuch. Since this man was returning after having worshiped in Jerusalem, we can assume he was Jewish. Nevertheless, Philip opened his eyes to the gospel and he was baptized. At this point in the life of the Church, the gospel had been proclaimed only to Jews and the half-Jew Samaritans. The missionary efforts of Philip and those who went out as he did accomplished a number of important things for the Church.

1. It proclaimed the story of Jesus and the message of the love of God in Jesus Christ.
2. It brought healing. Christianity has never been a thing of words only.
3. It brought, as a natural consequence, a joy that the Samaritans had never known before. A counterfeit

Christianity brings an atmosphere of gloom; the real thing radiates joy.

Peter and Cornelius. The second big change in the Church occurred through Peter. Peter was not prepared for what God had in store for him. After he returned from Samaria, he was praying on a rooftop when the Holy Spirit directed him to follow two men to the house of a Gentile named Cornelius (see Acts 10). The Book of Acts reveals several things about Cornelius:

1. Cornelius was a Roman centurion stationed at Caesarea, the headquarters of the government of Palestine. These centurions were the backbone of the Roman army. An ancient historian describes the qualifications of the centurion like this: "Centurions are desired not to be overbold and reckless so much as good leaders, of steady and prudent mind, not prone to take the offensive to start fighting wantonly, but able when overwhelmed and hard-pressed to stand fast and die at their posts." Cornelius therefore was a man who first and foremost knew what courage and loyalty were.

2. Cornelius was a God-fearer. In the first century this had become a technical term for Gentiles who, weary of the gods, the immoralities, and the frustration of their ancestral faiths, had attached themselves to the Jewish religion. They did not accept circumcision and the law, but they attended the synagogue and they believed in one God and in the ethics of the Jewish religion. Cornelius then was a man who was seeking after God, and as he sought God, God found him.

3. Cornelius was a man given to charity. He was characteristically kind. His search for God had made him

love men and he who loves his fellow men is not far from the Kingdom.

4. Cornelius was a man of prayer. Perhaps he did not clearly know the God to whom he prayed, but according to the light he had, he lived close to God.

Still, Cornelius was a Gentile and it was forbidden for a religious Jew to associate with a Gentile or visit with him. Because Peter was obedient to the Spirit of God, he learned that God's plan of salvation is for all people in all places, regardless of their race or origin. As he told Cornelius about Jesus, the Holy Spirit was poured out on Cornelius and his household. Since God had confirmed their acceptance through the Holy Spirit, Peter could not withhold water baptism from them and he ordered them baptized in the name of Jesus.

The point to the story of Cornelius is, first, we learn that God accepts all peoples, Jew and Gentile alike. Second, Peter learns that Jesus and the gospel are not reserved exclusively for the Jews. Strict adherence to Jewish law prohibited a Jew from having a close relationship with the Gentiles. The prohibition went so far as to refuse a Gentile woman help with her childbirth. Through Cornelius, God taught Peter of His love for the Gentile.

The Mission to Antioch. In the meantime, others of the Church traveled to Phoenicia, Cyprus, and Antioch. Mostly, they preached the gospel to the Jews in that area, but some of the men from Cyprus and Cyrene went to Antioch and spoke to the Greeks in that city. Acts 11:21 tells us, *"And the hand of the Lord was with them: and a great number believed, and turned unto the Lord."* These short accounts—Philip's trip into Samaria, Peter's visit to Cornelius, and the travels into Greece—tell the greatest events in history. Now, for the first time, the gospel is deliberately preached to the Gentiles. Everything has been working up to this end. There are three steps on the ladder. First, Philip preached to the Samaritans, which started the bridge to span the gap between the Jew and the Gentile. Second, Peter extended the bridge to Cornelius, a God-fearing Gentile, who was on the fringe of Judaism. Third, in Antioch the Church did not wait to be approached by Gentiles seeking admission. There they preached the gospel to the Gentiles and Christianity was finally launched on its worldwide mission.

Day Five

Part One

The Cost of Kingdom Work

As we enter this fifth and final segment, we have come a long way in answering the question: "What are we supposed to be doing as a Church?"

We began by identifying the *Ecclesia*, the Church within. Then we explored the organization of the *Koinonia*, a community of the redeemed. We identified the true ministers of the Church, upon whose shoulders the major work of the Church rests. We also examined the way in which these ministers were empowered for the work God called them to do. We went through the process whereby officers of the Church were appointed to help the pastors resolve conflicts within the community. Finally, we took a look at life within the community, prayer, responsibility, and reward; the fourth section gave us insight into the activity of the Church, both within and without.

The one problem we have not addressed is the matter of financing the community. In the beginning, those who

were a part of the *Ecclesia* divested themselves of all
"worldly goods" and gave the proceeds to the leaders to
be used for the good of the community. No pastor who
values his safety would propose such a resolution to the
Church today. Through the years the Church has been
lulled into a variety of techniques or gimmicks for financing the programs of the Church. The practice has ranged
from fund-raising anniversaries to marketing and selling.
Dinners, rummage sales, raffles, and drawings, even
door-to-door begging, are used as a means of encourag-
ing "giving." Such activities weaken the ministry of the
Church more than any outside negative influence. God
has always had one plan for financing His work throughout history. There is no principle in the Bible that is
more consistent than God's plan of financing His work.
The method was the *tithe*.

The Biblical Tithe

The Hebrew word for tithe is *maaser* (pronounced:
ma-a-ser). It comes from the Hebrew root *aser*, which
means "ten." In its final form, *maaser*, it means "tenth
of." The custom of paying a tithe was an ancient practice
found among many nations of the ancient world.

The biblical practice of giving a tenth of income or
property occurs before the time of Moses. The first recorded instance of tithing in the Bible occurs in Genesis
14:17-20. After rescuing Lot and defeating his enemies,
Abraham was met by Melchizedek, the "king of Salem"
and "priest of the most high God." The text states simply
that Abraham gave Melchizedek a tithe of all the goods he
had obtained in battle. There is no demand of Abraham

to give this tenth. Neither is there an explanation given about why Abraham gave a tithe to Melchizedek.

Jacob promises that he would give to God a tenth of all he received from God. Jacob said, "And this stone, which I have set for a pillar, shall be God's house: and of all that thou shalt give me I will surely give the tenth unto Thee" (Gen. 28:22).

The law of Moses outlined the practice of tithing in some detail. Leviticus 27:30-32 stated that the tithe of the land would include the seed of the land and the fruit of the tree. In addition, the people were required to set apart every tenth animal of their herds and flocks to the Lord.

Mosaic legislation on tithing is also found in two other passages. Numbers 18:21-32 stated that the tithes in Israel would be given to the Levites because the Levites did not receive an inheritance of land like the other tribes of Israel did. The Levites, for their tithe, were to offer a heave offering to the Lord. This constituted a tithe (10 percent) of the tithe they received from the other tribes. The balance of the tithe (the remaining 90 percent) was their income for the work they did as priests of the tabernacle.

A third passage dealing with the tithe is Deuteronomy 12:5-7,11-12,17-18. This passage instructed Israel to take their tithes to the place the Lord prescribes. This place later became the city of Jerusalem. In Deuteronomy, only a vegetable tithe is mentioned. In Second Chronicles 31:6, however, the tithe of cattle is mentioned.

In Deuteronomy 26:12-15, the third year is called the year of tithing. Apparently in this year only the goods given as tithes could be offered and stored locally. The offering of the tithe also took the form of a ritual meal (see Deut. 12:7,12). Some suggest that there were three tithes, but this seems unlikely. There is no mention of a tithe in Exodus, but there is a mention of the giving of the "firstfruits" (i.e., Ex. 23:16; see also Ezek. 44:29-30). Finally, the prophet Malachi proclaimed that Israel had robbed God in withholding tithes and offerings. Thus the Israelites were exhorted to bring their tithes into the storehouse in order to enjoy the Lord's blessing (see Mal. 3:8-12).

In the Old Testament the purpose of giving a tenth was to meet the material need of the Levite, the stranger, the fatherless (the orphan), and the widow (see Deut. 26:12-13). The tithe was an expression of gratitude to God by His people. Basically, the tithe was a way for the people to acknowledge God's ownership of everything in the earth.

The Tithe in the New Testament

In the New Testament the words *tithe* and *tithing* appear only eight times. In each of these passages the discussion of the tithe refers to the tithe as prescribed in the laws of the Old Testament.

Jesus in Matthew 23:23 observed that tithing was practiced, but that other godly practices had been neglected. Of these practices Jesus said, "these ought ye to have done," referring to judgment, mercy, and faith. He went on to admonish them "not to leave the other undone," meaning that they should continue to tithe.

In the writings of Paul, Peter, James, John, and the other New Testament writers, the subject of tithing is seldom mentioned. We can assume there was little need to address this subject, since the early church gave as much as required to meet the needs of the community.

And when they had prayed, the place was shaken where they were assembled together; and they were all filled with the Holy Ghost, and they spake the word of God with boldness. And the multitude of them that believed were of one heart and of one soul: neither said any of them that aught of the things which he possessed was his own; but they had all things common. And with great power gave the apostles witness of the resurrection of the Lord Jesus: and great grace was upon them all. Neither was there any among them that lacked: for as many as were possessors of lands or houses sold them, and brought the prices of the things that were sold, and laid them down at the apostles' feet: and distribution was made unto every man according as he had need. And Joses, who by the apostles was surnamed Barnabas, (which is, being interpreted, The son of consolation,) a Levite, and of the country of Cyprus, having land, sold it, and brought the money, and laid it at the apostles' feet (Acts 4:31-37).

Financing for the Church

The financing of the Church is through tithes and offerings. This is not to be done on a legalistic basis, though. It is giving because a giving God has given freely to us. He sends us into His Kingdom to reap fruit for Him by investing our time, our talent, and our treasures.

Once a man gave his two sons six ears of corn. He said to them, "This is food for your families when the winter comes."

The first son took his corn, carefully wrapped it, then placed it into the freezer, to remain until winter. When winter came he took out his corn, thawed it, and prepared a meal for his family.

The second son took his corn and dried the ears. Then he took the kernels from the corn and planted a garden. He carefully dug his trenches and dropped a few kernels of corn every five or six inches. In the fall, he harvested his corn and filled his freezer with the fruit of his harvest. He had enough to feed his family all winter long.

Both sons were given corn. The corn was seed. The first son took the seed his father gave him and tried to make the seed fit his need. The second son treated the corn as seed, planted it, and waited until the harvest could meet his need.

Tithing is "seed planting." The parable given by Jesus in Matthew 25:14-30 contains some very practical rules for financial stewardship:

Rule #1: The goods consigned to the servant (steward) belonged to the master.

(a) Tithing admits that all which one has received is from God.

(b) The purpose of the consignment is to equip us to work for Him.

(c) By His grace, we are stewards and temporary users of His goods.

Rule #2: The amount of goods consigned was based on the master's evaluation of the ability of each servant.

(a) Everyone had at least one talent.

(b) All did not receive the same.

But all these worketh that one and the selfsame Spirit, dividing to every man severally as he will (1 Corinthians 12:11).

Rule #3: Each servant was given full authority for handling the goods consigned to him.

(a) We are spiritual businessmen for the Lord.

(b) We are to use our God-given ability and use the goods consigned.

Rule #4: Each is called upon to give a strict accounting.

(a) When the accounting will take place is uncertain.

(b) It is certain that we will eventually give an accounting.

Rule #5: Each servant was required to show a gain.

Rule #6: Unproductive stewards suffered two judgments.

(a) What talent they had was taken away.

(b) They were cast into outer darkness.

In conclusion, tithing was not de-emphasized in the New Testament as some have supposed. The apostles inspired the first Church to give according as the Church had need. The response to that need led them to sell all they had and lay it at the apostles feet.

Day Five

Part Two

Stewardship of God's Provisions

Tithing in the Church Today

The church that does not take "tithing" seriously will always be a struggling and troubled church. God has no other program for financing His work than tithes and offerings. Tithing is not just about the giving of money. It is about the stewardship of God's provision.

The Greek word *oikonomos* (pronounced: ohee-ko-no-mos) means "the manager of a household or estate" (*oikos*, "a house"; *nemo*, "to arrange") or "a steward."

There is an interesting story behind the word *steward*. The word comes from Elizabethan English and is a contraction of two words, *sty* and *wart*. Sty meant a place where pigs were kept. Wart meant the person who was a sty keeper, a sty watcher, or a person who was a keeper of the pigs. As time passed, the steward became the one who took care of all of the owner's business while the owner was absent. An English family bearing the name

Stuart became the ruling family of England, which lifted the word from a pigpen to a kingdom.

Jesus lifts us from the pigpen to a place of managing His household. The Greek word *oikonomos* is also the root for the word *economy*. The spiritual implication of stewardship goes far beyond managing the Master's household. When we are lifted into God's spiritual realm we become stewards, but we must also be "committed" stewards. As spiritual stewards, we must commit our mind, soul, body, talents, vocation, avocation, home, and children to the Lordship of Jesus Christ. This commitment to the Lordship of Jesus the Christ means that we see our goods as His goods and we share these goods with the lost, the last, and the least.

This commitment should not be based on what the law prescribes. Legalistic approaches to Christian practices always lead to wrong conclusions. Stewardship obligations are accepted and practiced because a loving God has demonstrated His love through the gift of His Son Jesus Christ. We give of our time, our talents, and our treasures as a way of saying "thank you" to a God who has spared nothing in demonstrating His love for us. If in discussing stewardship we focus on tithes only, we are merely touching the tip of the iceberg. If we are to be good stewards then, we must be stewards over all of the Master's business. If we are to give of our time, talent, and treasures to God, then it must be in every area of "the work of the Church."

My commitment extends to evangelism, prayer, church leadership training, educating disciples, the cause of missions (domestic and foreign), and the commitment of mind and body. Simply stated, I am committed to devote my life to God and His business.

Material Possessions and the Tithe

And Jesus looked round about, and saith unto His disciples, How hardly shall they that have riches enter into the kingdom of God! And the disciples were astonished at His words. But Jesus answereth again, and saith unto them, Children, how hard is it for them that trust in riches to enter into the kingdom of God! It is easier for a camel to go through the eye of a needle, than for a rich man to enter into the kingdom of God. And they were astonished out of measure, saying among themselves, Who then can be saved? And Jesus looking upon them saith, With men it is impossible, but not with God: for with God all things are possible (Mark 10:23-27).

Jesus looked round and said to His disciples, "With what difficulty will those who have money enter into the Kingdom of God!" His disciples were amazed at His words. Jesus repeated, "Children, how difficult it is for those who trust in money to enter into the Kingdom of God! It is easier for a camel to go through the eye of a needle than for a rich man to enter the Kingdom of God." They were exceedingly astonished. "Who then," they said to Him, "can be saved?" Jesus looked at them and said, "With man it is impossible, but not with God. All things are possible with God."

The young ruler refused the challenge of Jesus and walked sorrowfully away (see Mk. 10:17-22). No doubt the eyes of Jesus and of the company of the apostles followed him until his figure faded into the distance. Then

Jesus turned and looked round at His own men. "How very difficult it is," He said, "for a man who has money to enter into the Kingdom of God." (The word used for money is *chremata*, which is defined by Aristotle as "all those things of which the value is measured by coinage.") We may wonder why this saying astonished the disciples. Twice we are told of their amazement. They were amazed because Jesus was turning accepted Jewish standards completely upside down. Popular Jewish morality was simple. It believed that prosperity was the sign of a good man. If a man was rich, God must have honored and blessed him. Wealth was proof of excellence of character and of favor with God. The Psalmist sums it up: "I have been young, and now am old; yet have I not seen the righteous forsaken, nor his seed begging bread" (Ps. 37:25).

No wonder the disciples were surprised! They surely thought that the more prosperous a man was, the more certain he could be of entering the Kingdom. To clarify His point, Jesus repeated His thought in a slightly different way, saying, "How difficult it is for those who have put their trust in riches to enter the Kingdom." No one saw the dangers of prosperity and of material things more clearly than Jesus did. What are these dangers?

1. Material possessions tend to fix a man's heart to this world. He has so large a stake in it, he has so great an interest in it, that it is difficult for him to think beyond his earthly existence. It is especially difficult for him to contemplate leaving it. Dr. Johnson was once shown round a famous castle and the lovely grounds surrounding it. After he had seen it all, he turned to his friends

and said, "These are the things that make it difficult to die."[1] The danger of possessions is that they fix a man's thoughts and interests to this world.

2. If a man's main interest is in material possessions, it tends to make him think of everything in terms of price. A shepherd's wife wrote a most interesting letter to a newspaper. Her children had been brought up in the loneliness of the hills. They were simple and unsophisticated. Then her husband got a position in town and the children were introduced to a new life style. They changed dramatically—and they changed for the worse. The last paragraph of her letter read, "Which is preferable for a child's upbringing—a lack of worldliness, but with better manners and sincere and simple thoughts, or worldliness and its present-day habit of knowing the price of everything and the true value of nothing?"[2] If a man's main interest is in material things, he will think in terms of price and not in terms of value. He will think in terms of what money can get. He may well forget there are values in this world that money cannot buy, things that have no price, because they are too precious to set a price on them. It is fatal when a man begins to think that everything worth having has a price.

3. Jesus would have said that the possession of material things is two things:

1.   *Sermon Illustrations for Windows*, by NAVPRESS, P.O. Box 6000, Colorado Springs, CO 80934. Used by permission.
2.   From *Dynamic Preaching*, a Publication of Seven Worlds Corporation, P.O. Box 11565, Knoxville, TN 37939. Used by permission.

(a) It is an acid test of a man. For 100 men who can stand adversity, only one can stand prosperity. Prosperity can so very easily make a man arrogant, proud, self-satisfied, and worldly. It takes a mature man to bear wealth worthily.

(b) It is a responsibility. A man will always be judged by two standards—how he got his possessions and how he uses them. The more he has, the greater the responsibility he has. Will he use what he has selfishly or generously? Will he use it as if he had undisputed possession of it, or will he remember he holds it in stewardship for God?

Based upon this teaching from Jesus, the reaction of the disciples was that salvation was well-nigh impossible. Then Jesus stated the whole doctrine of salvation in a nutshell. "If," He said, "salvation depended on a man's own efforts, it would be impossible for anyone. But salvation is the gift of God and all things are possible to Him."

The man who trusts in himself and in his possessions can never be saved. The man who trusts in the saving power and redeeming love of God can enter freely into salvation. This teaching from Jesus was also taught by Paul in letter after letter and it continues today to be the foundational message of the Christian faith.

Day Five

Part Three

Paul and Tithing

The Motivation for Tithing

Paul spoke of the manner in which the churches gave beyond the initial ten percent in his second letter to the church at Corinth. His message to the church sets the stage for future church giving and attitudes in giving.

Moreover, brethren, we do you to wit of the grace of God bestowed on the churches of Macedonia; how that in a great trial of affliction the abundance of their joy and their deep poverty abounded unto the riches of their liberality. For to their power, I bear record, yea, and beyond their power they were willing of themselves; praying us with much entreaty that we would receive the gift, and take upon us the fellowship of the ministering to the saints. And this they did, not as we hoped, but first gave their own selves to the Lord, and unto us by the will of God. Insomuch that we desired Titus, that as he had begun, so he would also finish in you the same grace also. Therefore, as ye abound in every thing, in faith, and

*utterance, and knowledge, and in all diligence, and in
your love to us, see that ye abound in this grace also*
(2 Corinthians 8:1-7).

One of the plans nearest to Paul's heart was the collection that he was organizing for the church of Jerusalem. This was the mother church, but she was poor. It
was Paul's desire for all the Gentile churches to remember and help the church that was their mother in the
faith. He reminded the Corinthians (and the Church of
today) of their duty and urges them to generosity. He
uses five arguments to appeal to them to give worthily.

1. He cites the example of others. He tells them how
generous the Macedonian churches had been. They
were poor and in trouble, but they gave all they had,
which was far more than anyone expected. At the Feast
of Purim there is a regulation that, however poor a man
is, he must find someone poorer than himself and give
him a gift. Those who are wealthy are not always the
most generous. Often those who have the least to give
are more ready to give. There is a common saying, "It is
the poor who help the poor," because they know what
poverty is like.

2. He cites the example of Jesus Christ. For Paul, the
sacrifice of Jesus did not begin on the cross. It did not
even begin with His birth. It began in Heaven, when He
laid His glory aside and consented to come to earth.
Paul's challenge to the Christian is, "With that tremendous example of generosity before you, how can you
hold back?"

3. He cites their own past record. They have been
foremost in everything. Can they then lag behind in this?

If men were only true to their own highest standards, if we all lived always at our best, what a difference it would make!

4. He stresses the necessity of putting good feelings into action. The Corinthians had been the first to receive this kind of appeal. But a feeling that remains only a feeling, a pity that remains a pity only of the heart, a fine desire that never turns into a find deed, is a sadly truncated and frustrated thing. So often the tragedy of life is not that we have no high impulses, but that we fail to turn them into actions.

5. He reminds them that life has a strange way of balancing accounts. Far more often than not we find that God's gifts are measured to us with the same measure as we measure to others. Life has a way of repaying bounty with bounty, and the sparing spirit with the sparing spirit. Paul compliments the Macedonians for the way in which they discharged their responsibility in giving.

Two men stand out in the sacrificial way they gave. Aristarchus of Thessalonica was with Paul on the last journey to Rome (see Acts 27:2). Paul was under arrest and on his way to trial before the emperor. There was only one way in which Aristarchus could accompany him and that was as Paul's slave. Aristarchus in the fullest sense gave himself.

The second man was Epaphroditus. During Paul's last days in prison, he came to Paul with a gift from Philippi. Then, while with Paul in prison, he fell grievously ill. Paul said of him, "he nearly died for the work of Christ" (see Phil. 2:26-30). No gift can be a gift in any real sense unless the giver gives with it a bit of himself. That is why personal giving is always the best kind. Jesus gave all that He had, His life, and He is the supreme example.

Paul concludes this discussion in Second Corinthians 8 with a quotation from Exodus 16:18 that tells how, when the Israelites gathered the manna in the wilderness, whether a man gathered little or much, it was enough.

Day Five

Part Four

Stewardship, Service, and Judgment

Preaching and Practical Service

If any man speak, let him speak as the oracles of God; if any man minister, let him do it as of the ability which God giveth: that God in all things may be glorified through Jesus Christ, to whom be praise and dominion for ever and ever. Amen (1 Peter 4:11).

Peter is thinking of the two great activities of the Christian church: preaching and practical service. The word he uses for "sayings" is *logia*. This Greek word is often used to describe the words from gods or God. The heathen used it for the oracles that came to them from their gods and the Christians used it for the words of Scripture and the words of Christ. So Peter is saying, "If a man has the duty of preaching, let him preach not as one offering his own opinions or propagating his own prejudices, but as one with a message from God."

It was said of one great preacher: "First he listened to God, and then he spoke to men." It was said of another that ever and again he paused, "as if listening for a voice." There lies the secret of preaching power.

Peter goes on to say that if a Christian is engaged in practical service, he must render that service in the strength that God supplies. It is as if he said, "When you are engaged in Christian service, you must not do it as if you were conferring a personal favor or distributing bounty from your own store, but being fully aware that what you give you first received from God." Such an attitude preserves the giver from pride and the receiver from humiliation.

The aim is to glorify God in all that we do and with every offering we bring. Preaching is not done to display the preacher, but to bring men face to face with God. Service is rendered not to bring prestige to the supplier, but to turn men's thoughts to God. E.G. Selwyn reminds us that the motto of the great Benedictine order of monks is four letters, I-O-G-D, which stands for the Latin words *in omnibus glorificetur Deus* (in order that in all things God may be glorified). A new grace and glory would enter the Church if all believers ceased doing things for themselves and did them for God.

Accounting and Judgment

Paul thinks of himself and his fellow preachers as stewards of the secrets that God desires to reveal to His own people. The steward (*oikonomos*) was the major domo. He was in charge of the whole administration of the house or the estate; he controlled the staff; and he issued the supplies. Still, regardless of how much he controlled the household staff, he was still a slave where the master was concerned. Whatever position in the Church a man may hold, whatever power he may wield, and whatever prestige he may enjoy, he still remains the servant of Christ.

That brings Paul to the thought of judgment. The one thing that an *oikonomos* must be is reliable. The very fact that he enjoys so much independence and responsibility makes it all the more necessary that his master be able to depend upon him without concern for his performance. The Corinthian church was split into various sects. Each sect had leaders (masters) and the members of a sect would judge the leaders, preferring one to the other. So Paul speaks of three judgments that every man must face.

1. He must face the judgment of his fellow men. In this case Paul says that is nothing to him, but there is a sense in which a man cannot disregard the judgment of his fellow men. The odd thing is, in spite of occasional mistakes, the judgment of our fellow man is often right. Why? Every man instinctively admires the basic qualities of honor, honesty, reliability, generosity, sacrifice, and love. Antisthenes, the Cynic philosopher, used to say, "There are only two people who can tell you the truth about yourself—an enemy who has lost his temper and a friend who loves you dearly."

Nevertheless, we should not allow the judgment of men to influence us so much that we fail to do what we believe to be right. At the same time, the judgment of men is often more accurate than we would like to think because of the instincts just mentioned above.

2. Leaders must face their own self-judgment. Once again Paul discounts this concept. Paul knew that anyone who judged his own performance often erred because of self-satisfaction, pride, and conceit. Still, I believe every man must face his own judgment. One of the basic laws of Greek ethics was, "Man, know thyself." The Cynics insisted that one of the first characteristics of a real man was "the ability to get on with himself." A man cannot get away from himself and if he loses his self-respect, life becomes an intolerable thing.

3. He must face the judgment of God. In the final analysis this is the only judgment that counts. The judgment Paul awaited was not that of any man-made day of judgment, but the judgment of the Day of the Lord. God's is the final judgment for two reasons:

(a) Only God knows all the circumstances. He knows the struggles a man has had; He knows the secrets that a man can tell to no one; and He knows the depths a man has sunk to and the heights a man had achieved.

(b) Only God knows all the motives. "Man sees the deed, but God sees the intention." Many a deed that looks noble may have been done from the most selfish and ignoble of motives. Many a deed that seems to be without merit may have been done with the highest of motives. He and only He, who made the human heart, knows it and can judge it. We would do well to remember two things: first, even if we escape all other judgments or shut our eyes to them, we cannot escape the judgment of God; and second, judgment belongs to God and we would do well not to judge any man.

Day Five

Part Five

Final Things

During this final part of our seminar presentation, we offer a few parting words to all of our seminar participants. As a reader, you have received all of the information that the participants of our seminars enjoy. The only disadvantage for you is missing out on the daily fellowship and sharing with the seminar groups and participating in the casual talk that always takes place during the breaks. It is my hope that you will be moved by what you have read to seek out one of our seminars. As a seminar participant, you will be strengthened through the interaction and will build on what you have learned in this book as well.

At the end of the five-day seminar, I close my lectures and the final session by presenting the participants with a series of charts that act as a summary of the material we have covered. I call these charts the "Challenge of the Pies." I am including these at the end of this book for you to consider as you ponder the information you have read.

In closing, let me offer my prayer and my blessing for you and your family. I know that you will benefit from this information, if you take the time to put these principles to work in your life. In the churches that I have had the privilege of presenting this information, the pastors tell me they have noticed a profound change in the level of participation from their membership. I can only hope that these words will penetrate your heart and mind as you go about the precious life you have through our Lord Jesus Christ.

Church work and the work of the Church will be fully supported by the members of the body in relationship to their dedication to God. Stewardship involves commitment to the Body of Christ. You must be determined to give of your time, talent, and treasures that God's love may be shared throughout the world.

The Work of the Church

And Jesus came and spake unto them, saying, All power is given unto Me in heaven and in earth. Go ye therefore, and teach all nations, baptizing them in the name of the Father, and of the Son, and of the Holy Ghost: Teaching them to observe all things whatsoever I have commanded you: and, lo, I am with you alway, even unto the end of the world. Amen (Matthew 28:18-20).

But ye shall receive power, after that the Holy Ghost is come upon you: and ye shall be witnesses unto Me both in Jerusalem, and in all Judaea, and in Samaria, and unto the uttermost part of the earth (Acts 1:8).

Pie #1: The Work of the Church

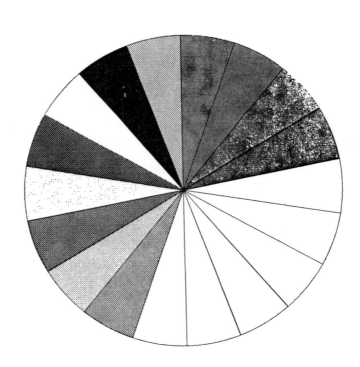

The Work Of The Church

Pie #2: Church Work

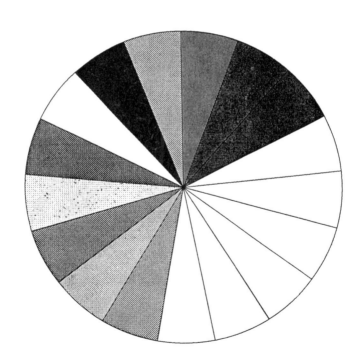

Church Work

How Does Pie #1 Relate to Pie #2?

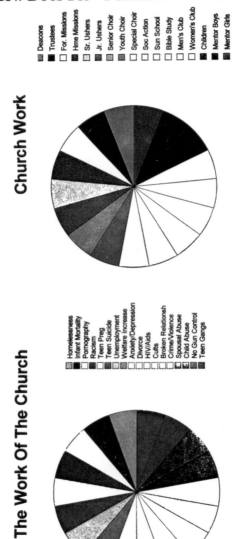

Church Work

Deacons
Trustees
For. Missions
Hme Missions
Sr. Ushers
Jr. Ushers
Senior Choir
Youth Choir
Special Choir
Soc Action
Sun School
Bible Study
Men's Club
Women's Club
Children
Mentor Boys
Mentor Girls

The Work Of The Church

Homelessness
Infant Mortality
Pornography
Racism
Teen Preg
Teen Suicide
Unemployment
Welfare Increase
Anxiety/Depression
Divorce
HIV/Aids
Cults
Broken Relationsh
Crime/Violence
Spousal Abuse
Child Abuse
No Gun Control
Teen Gangs